CONNECT

THROUGH

EMOTIONAL INTELLIGENCE

Learn to Master Self, Understand Others,
and Build Strong, Productive
Relationships

D0876539

MIKE ACKER

ISBN: 978-1-954024-19-9 Hardcover
        978-1-954024-20-5 Paperback
        978-1-954024-21-2 Ebook

https://www.advantage-publishing.com

To contact, please e-mail: contact@mikeacker.com

READ FIRST

Thank you for investing in my book.

As an appreciation, I'd love to give you access to free content.

Self-awareness Work Pages

This downloadable PDF comes from the *Connect through Emotional Intelligence Workbook*. These pages provide you an outline to assess your Emotional Intelligence to provide you with a better picture of your journey.

In addition, this site contains free content from my other books, which hundreds of people have accessed to gain confidence and clarity in their communication and leadership.

Visit this link or use the QR code for your free gift:
https://content.mikeacker.com

DEDICATION

This book is dedicated to Steve Gutzler.

*What began with a speaking gig, turned into
a friendship and partnership.*

Without your influence and encouragement, this book would not exist.

CONTENTS

INTRODUCTION

Do you remember your first "professional" job? For me, it was a leadership role that involved organizing teams. I was twenty-two, fresh out of college, and eager to prove myself. Like any newbie, I did some things really well but also made some really big mistakes. About a year in, I'd just completed my biggest project to date. In hindsight, it had gone reasonably well, but all I could see were all the ways it had fallen short of my expectations. I felt overworked, underappreciated, and completely fried. I was running on fumes and was not thinking clearly. Ever been there?

My manager, Tony, called me into his office. My guard was up before I even knocked on his door. We started talking about the project, and I began venting all my frustrations. I complained about everything that had gone wrong and blamed anyone I could—not a great way to start. But then I started to attack *him* and his involvement in the project. I still cringe when I think about it.

I finally stopped talking and somewhere, in the back of my head, I started to think, *Oh shoot.*

Tony smiled paternally and said, "You know, Mike, it's been a long week. Why don't you take the rest of the day off and we'll chat tomorrow?"

I went home and crashed on my second-hand mattress. I came back the next day and headed straight to his office to apologize. I knew that I'd been out of line. In hindsight, he had every right to let me go.

"Hey, Tony…"

He held his hand up. "Yesterday, you were tired and disappointed," he said. "Those aren't a great combination. I could see you needed some rest. Feeling better now?"

"Yeah, thanks," I said, and we proceeded to have a productive debriefing.

Tony demonstrated Emotional Intelligence. I had not.

WHAT IS EMOTIONAL INTELLIGENCE?

Have you ever known someone who was incredibly bright or exceptionally gifted and just killed it when they worked alone, but working with or—worse yet—*for* them was a nightmare? Another example: Have you ever watched *Big Bang Theory*? The show's whole "brilliant but socially awkward" trope is based on the fact that someone can have a very high IQ but seem almost incapable of cultivating healthy interactions with others. It makes for hilarious gags but is no joke in real life.

What IQ is to the brain, Emotional Intelligence (or EI, as we'll call it) is to the heart. In their seminal research in 1990, psychologists Dr. Peter Salovey and Dr. John Mayer introduced the term EI. They described it as "the ability to engage in sophisticated information processing about one's own and others' emotions and the ability to use this information as a guide to thinking and behavior."[1]

Said another way—your EI represents your relative ability to choose the wisest course of action based on your judgment of your emotions as well as the emotions of others. Tony's high EI allowed him to understand that I was tired and frustrated and therefore lacked the emotional reserves or perspective to debrief. He was then able to make a sound judgment and choose a wise course of action. My low EI prevented me from understanding my and my team's emotional state which drove a foolish course of action.

Take a moment and think about these three qualifications for success in any job:

- Intelligence

- Skills/training

- Emotional Intelligence

Which one of these would you guess has the highest impact on success? Second highest? Third? In the professional world, our primary focus tends to be on IQ first, then on skills. Only

---

[1] "Emotional Intelligence: New Ability or Eclectic Traits?" John D. Mayer, Peter Salovey and David R. Caruso. *American Psychologist*, September 2008, Vol. 63, No. 6, pages 503-517.

recently have we started putting EI on the list, but psychologists have discovered that EI is actually *more important* than IQ.

Historically, our culture has focused on academic intelligence as the most important predictor of personal success. But there's far more to it than that. In fact, research shows that academic intelligence, what we typically call IQ, is responsible for predicting only about 20 percent of someone's success.[2] The remaining 80 percent represents factors such as the family that person is born into, sheer luck, and, you guessed it, EI. Students who are academically successful may be driven to do well on tests. They have clearly found a way to excel in their academic systems but that doesn't necessarily lead to doing well later on in life. This is especially true if these systems are no longer part of their everyday experience.

In his groundbreaking book *Frames of Mind*, Harvard Psychologist Dr. Howard Gardner encouraged movement away from the sole reliance of academic intelligence, suggesting there are many different types of intelligence, including: kinesthetic (key for athletic competition), spatial (architecture, design, or engineering), musical, naturalist (understanding the natural world), *inter*personal (understanding others and forming meaningful connections), and *intra*personal (understanding and controlling our own emotions and behaviors). Gardner's work revealed that human intelligence is far more complex than previously realized.

All that to say, IQ is far too narrow a measurement to predict overall success in life. A better indicator is high EI: being self-

---

[2] Goleman, *Emotional Intelligence*, 34.

motivated, having the ability to handle and navigate adversity, understanding oneself, being able to connect and empathize with others, and having a persistent sense of hope.

HOW'S YOUR EI?

Really, how is your EI? There are many online assessments, of varying quality, that you can look into or you can use these questions as a guide. Don't treat them as yes/no questions but as a way to start an internal conversation.

- How "in touch" are you with your emotions?

- How easily can you figure out why you feel what you feel?

- Do you understand and appreciate both your strengths and weaknesses?

- How long does it take for you to recover from a distressing emotion?

- How easily are you able to adapt to changes?

- Can you sense how other people are feeling and understand their point of view?

- How are you at negotiating conflict?

- How well do you work on a team?

We're all quite apt at self-deceit, so if you want a better assessment of your EI, ask someone you trust to answer these questions about you. EI is gauged by how comfortable we are with our own emotions as well as how we interact with others—so an outside perspective is invaluable.

YOU CAN'T AFFORD TO IGNORE YOUR EI

Since Salovey and Mayer's work in 1990, EI has been the subject of a great deal of research, and we continue to learn that EI is central to success at every level—in your work, in your relationships, and in your own health. Taking your own EI seriously is critical for your personal wellbeing and your ability to make and maintain healthy connections with others. Failing to do so can be disastrous.

THE BENEFITS OF A HIGH EI

The benefits of having a high EI are far-reaching, and well-documented:[3]

- Better personal health and self-awareness.

- Ability to separate other people's actions from your reactions.

- Better control of your own emotions and actions.

- Greater impulse control and focus.

- Improved ability to handle stressful situations.

---

[3] Goleman, *Emotional Intelligence*, pp. 283–84.

- Healthier personal and professional relationships.

- Ability to identify other people's emotions and understand their perspective (more important now than ever!).

- Lowering negative behavior and increasing healthy behavior in others.

When you operate with a high EI, you are better equipped to collaborate with others, making you a valued asset to the entire team. This leads to promotions at work, more leadership opportunities, improved relationships, and greater overall joy in life.

THE COST OF A LOW EI

A low EI is costly to our well-being, our relationships, and our work. Instead of studies, I want you to see it in action. Nick was a top performer long before I met him. He managed a large boat dealership on the east coast and business was booming under his leadership. I mean booming! He was making a lot of money for the owners. But that couldn't protect him from his own low EI. He was fired because of his inability to control his anger, which had created a terrible work environment. The owners had been forced to choose between Nick and the rest of the team.

Nick had to move several states away to California and start over. He pooled his resources and founded his own dealership. No one could fire him now! He created an enormously successful business that soon spanned five locations. And Nick's success reached beyond just those who came to his dealerships. He was establishing meaningful connections and investing in the local community. But then, things began to unravel. Employees were leaving faster than he could replace them. He'd try to persuade former staff members to return, but they refused. He started hiring personal friends, but they, too, kept leaving. Now he wasn't just losing employees, he was losing friends.

The issue? Nick's low EI, particularly his anger issues. Without any ability to control his own emotional response to the inevitable challenges of business, Nick frequently lost his temper. He'd shout at his staff and berate them for mistakes instead of working towards effective solutions. It didn't matter how good the money was, no one was willing to be treated like that. Nick's business acumen was clear—he was a phenomenal salesperson and an experienced business strategist—but none of it could overcome his low EI.

Like many of us, Nick was profoundly shaped by his childhood experiences. He was surrounded by adults who took their anger out on one another in harmful ways, and he was the victim of things I wouldn't wish on my worst enemy. Because he hadn't addressed the past and the resulting low EI, Nick's failed to thrive. But even as his business closed, an unexpected personal event gave Nick a second chance, and now he's learning to interact in healthier ways. No matter how low our Emotional Intelligence is, it's never too late to grow!

Can you see how EI is a greater indicator of success than IQ or skills? Having a low EI is costly and refusing to address it will guarantee failure. Yes, Nick was shaped by his environment, but he didn't need to be a victim of it. He had no power over his past, but he had power over the present. This is true for all of us. When we fail to improve our EI, we do damage to ourselves *and* to others. But, when we can recognize and control our own emotions, we will find greater success in every aspect of our life. That's the goal of this book.

YOUR TURN

Your EI differs from IQ in a crucial way: nearly everyone has the capacity to vastly improve their EI.

In my first book, *Speak With No Fear*, I talk about growing up as a skinny white kid in Mexico. For years, I didn't feel like I belonged. Seven years later, I returned to the United States after finally acclimating to Mexico. Once again, I felt like an outsider. Never fitting in led me to improve my EI (before I had even heard of the term). First, by seeking to understand myself through reading, writing, and counseling. Then, by carefully studying others to develop my social skills, and finally, by giving me empathy for other outsiders. No matter how many schoolbooks I read, my IQ will never be as high as Albert Einstein's. But I've already vastly improved my EI and am still growing.

Let me ask you, why did you buy this book? Was it for yourself? Your team? Were you planning to leave it on your nightstand, hoping your partner would see it? (That's not a great strategy, by the way.) Whether you're an EI Einstein or dunce, I believe this book will help you:

- Understand your own emotions and their outcomes.

- Learn how to regulate emotions and motivate your actions.

- Better "read" those around you.

- Enjoy better working relationships.

- Discover areas of disconnection.

- Achieve better results in any field.

I promise that if you commit to studying this book, you will be on the road to improvement.

Here's the big picture of where we're going: Imagine that you and a bunch of friends are planning a week-long camping trip the next state over, involving about a dozen cars. Vehicle-wise, there are three key components for a safe journey:

1. You need to make sure that your car is running well and is capable of making the trip.

2. Once you're on the road, you need to interact safely with countless vehicles, watching for brake lights and anticipating erratic driving.

3. You need to coordinate with your friends to arrive at the same location.

I'll explain how these apply in just a moment, but first I want to return to the research done on EI. Six years after Salovey and Mayer's seminal work, Dr. Daniel Goleman brought the concept of EI to a much wider audience with his book *Emotional Intelligence.* Pulling from many different strands of research, Dr. Goleman defined Emotional Intelligence according to five areas of aptitude: self-awareness, self-regulation, self-motivation, social skills, and empathy. As Dr. Goleman put it: "My concern is with . . . abilities such as being able to motivate oneself and persist in the face of frustrations; to control impulse and delay gratification; to regulate one's moods and keep distress from swamping the ability to think; to empathize and to hope."[4]

Notice again these five aptitudes because they will provide some of our core topics:

- Self-awareness,

- Self-regulation,

- Self-motivation,

- Social skills, and

- Empathy.

The first three are all about yourself (*intra*personal intelligence). The second two are about others (*inter*personal intelligence). In this book, we'll begin by looking at you and how to make sound judgements about your own emotions and choose the wisest

---

[4] Goleman, *Emotional Intelligence,* 34.

course of action. Then, we'll look at how you interact with other people's emotions—responding to people in *general* then to those who are *part of your life*. So, the three parts of the book are:

1. Me: Understanding and controlling my own "car."

2. Them: Being able to read and safely interact with the other "cars."

3. Us: Interacting with the other "cars" in my group to arrive at our desired destination.

Think of this book as a toolbox that will not only help you fix your own car but also help with everyone else's cars. Each of these parts has three chapters, filled with research, stories, and useful information. But more than information, these chapters are devoted to helping you see real growth and increase your EI.

At the end of each chapter, you'll notice the "Applying Your EI" section. Don't miss these! These are specially prepared to help you put each lesson into practice and achieve noticeable growth. Some will require a bit of reflection, perhaps even talking with others and completing certain exercises with them.

After reading this book, you'll have a better grasp of how high EI can help you be a more effective leader, experience improvement in your work performance, and better connect with others.

A WORD OF WARNING

We all have books we fully intended to read, but they are now sitting on our shelf, gathering dust. EI is too important to be the victim of procrastination! The longer you wait to begin this work, the harder it will be when you finally start. So, whatever thing you're thinking about doing before starting this journey, write it on a list to be done *afterwards*. Trust me, you'll be thankful you did. And others will thank you, too!

That's enough introduction. Let's get going, together.

PART I: ME

CHAPTER 1:
SELF-AWARENESS

Healthy Emotional Intelligence starts with *self*. Returning to the car analogy, you need to make sure that your car is in good working condition before taking it out on the road. That's the focus of Part One. In this chapter, we'll focus on self-awareness—discovering what's under the hood. In Chapter 2, we'll discuss self-control—the brakes and steering wheel. And in Chapter 3, we'll look at self-motivation—the accelerator.

There was a restaurant manager who had just bought a brand-new Dodge SUV. He was so proud of the thing. He'd wash it every Saturday and wouldn't dream of taking it off-road. After a couple months, it started making a disturbing noise under the hood. At first, he ignored it, but then it just got worse.

He finally mentioned it to some of the guys at the restaurant and one of them said, "I know a thing or two about cars. Let me look at it."

The manager tossed him the keys and said, "I'll give you tomorrow off if you get it figured out."

He went out and opened the hood, then stared in disbelief. The engine compartment was completely filled with pinecones and acorns, hidden there by the neighborhood squirrels. The manager may not have known much about cars, but if he'd bothered popping the hood, even he could have figured out the problem!

When it comes to emotions, many people are afraid to pop the hood and look at what is going on underneath. It seems easier and safer to just ignore them. But what you don't know *can* hurt you—and those around you.

EMOTIONS MOVE YOU

When you hear the word "emotion," what's the first thing you think of? Feelings, probably. Maybe it's a specific feeling, like happy or sad. But, by and large, our first thought when we hear the word "emotion" is to think of something happening inside of us, something "under the hood."

The English word "emotion" comes from the Latin verb *emovere*—a combination of the prefix *ex* meaning "out" and *movere*, meaning "move." So, the root of our English word "emotion" comes from the Latin verb meaning to "move out" or "move away." It describes a movement, an action.

Emotions are your engine. They are what drive you and compel you to act. No matter how logical you think you are, emotions are still the driving force. As near as I can tell, the spectrum of human emotionality doesn't run from "high emotion" on one side to "no emotion" on the other, but from "uncontrolled emotion" to "repressed emotion," and either extreme is the mark of low EI. It is absolutely essential to understand them if you're to understand your actions and, ultimately, yourself.

EMOTIONAL MATURITY

As I said in the Introduction, having a high EI is even more important than a high IQ for determining success. This is especially true in areas of life where sheer intellectual aptitude isn't as relevant as other factors, such as in romantic relationships, friendships, leadership, and your personal health. Repeated surveys have shown that college students who graduate at the top of their class are not guaranteed to have the highest success later on in life. This theory is proven when those same graduates are tested again at middle age, and their results differ vastly from before. Even more than academic achievement, a high EI is key to determining one's overall health, happiness, and well-being.

REMEMBER:

A HIGH EI IS MORE IMPORTANT THAN A HIGH IQ.

Over the past couple decades, most U.S. states have instituted a "graduated driver's license programs." This means that new drivers will receive a license with restrictions on the number of other teenagers that are allowed in the car, etc. Over time, these restrictions drop off, providing the driver doesn't have any moving violations. These rules have already saved thousands of lives and protected countless more from getting hurt. If those rules would have been around when I was sixteen, I'm sure I would've thought them "unfair" and insisted that I was completely ready to drive—even though my three early "incidents" would suggest otherwise. Driving a car is very dangerous and requires a great deal of maturity.

Emotional Intelligence is emotional maturity. Understanding your own emotions, and those of others, is part of maturity—the more mature you are, the better equipped you are to deal with your full range of emotions and all that life brings your way. Yet, there are many adults out there who drive their "car" with the emotional maturity of a toddler behind the wheel of a Ferrari. Somebody is bound to get hurt.

Are you mature enough to drive your "car"? And what are the marks of maturity? *Psychology Today* names a few.[5] First, delayed gratification is a proven sign of maturity. There's a famous study from the 1970s called the Stanford marshmallow. In this experiment, children either received one small snack immediately or multiple snacks if they were willing to wait. Researchers found that the ability to delay gratification was linked to several other success indicators later in life. Choosing long-term success over short-term gains is a sure indicator of maturity—and this is true at any age.

---

[5] https://www.psychologytoday.com/us/blog/artificial-maturity/201211/the-marks-maturity. Accessed 2/19/2021

Second, mature people are teachable. They assume they always have something to learn, no matter how much they know or how old they are. Mature people seek counsel and allow their decisions to be informed and shaped by others' wisdom.

Third, mature people are consistently grateful. Those who regularly express gratitude focus on the big picture, rather than getting lost in the negative details of life.

Fourth, mature people are grounded in their sense of self—neither criticism nor praise can shake them from their grounded identity.

All these marks of maturity are necessary components to having a high EI.

NAME THE EMOTION

Like that restaurant manager, many of us are afraid to open the hood and examine the emotions underneath. However, being emotionally aware is key to having a high EI. It begins with recognizing your own emotions. You must be able to literally name them. The trouble is, we have a lot of different emotions, and they can be hard to distinguish at times.

One tool for naming the particular emotion you're experiencing is to recognize the general one, then narrow it down from there. Psychologist Dr. Robert Plutchik has spent years researching emotions, and he concludes that humans universally have eight primary emotions: joy, sadness, acceptance, disgust, fear, anger, surprise, and anticipation. These are the foundation for all emotions—and there are many! Emotions are often much more nuanced than we realize. But if you begin with these primary ones, you can narrow your feelings into a more specific subcategory of emotions. You can even find a subcategory within the first subcategory, and so on and so forth. Keep going until you have located the highly specific emotion you're experiencing. An Emotion Wheel, like the one below from Dr. Plutchik, can help you locate, identify, and name your precise emotion.

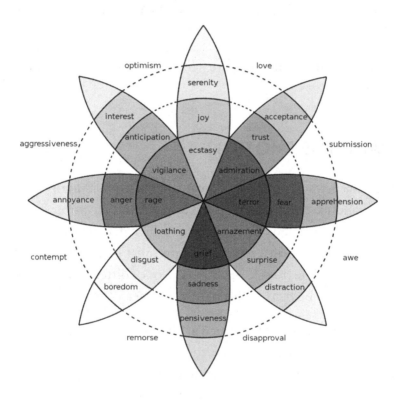

Figure 1 : The Plutchik Wheel of Emotions

For me, realizing the importance of naming my emotions came from counseling. I used to think therapy was for wimps or deeply troubled people. But then three influential mentors of mine shared their counseling experiences, and I thought, *if they can go to counselors and find help, maybe it would be helpful for me, too.*

In my twenties, I started a practice of going to a counselor for periodic check-ins. Kind of like a checkup for my car, I'd take myself to a professional to make sure everything was running properly. Later in my thirties, I began seeing a counselor more regularly to talk through some major changes in my life. Sitting together in his office, he asked how I felt. I didn't realize that he was, in a way, setting a trap.

"Angry," I said.

But he kept pushing me to narrow down my actual emotion.

Was I feeling let down? Humiliated? Bitter? Frustrated? Distant? Critical?

"Let down," I finally replied.

"Okay," he said. "So, are you feeling betrayed, resentful, misled, bitter?"

Through this back and forth process, he helped me realize that emotions are more specific than I'd thought. This has helped me in many ways—including how I communicate with my wife! I used to only express a few of my emotions: happy, sad, frustrated, etc. But those aren't specific enough to convey all that I feel and experience. It's like saying, "I went to Africa." Well, which part? The Saharan? Sub-Saharan? South? West?

Africa is *big*! And many of the countries there are big. Knowing *exactly* where you went in Africa will tell me much more about your experience. Being specific matters.

Using broad categories for emotions is like calling your mechanic and saying your car won't work. If you do that, the first thing they are going to do is help you narrow things down. "Is it an electrical problem?" they might ask. "Is the battery working?" "Does it start up okay?" "Does it die suddenly?" These questions help narrow down what's going on by identifying the specific issue causing your car problems. But you cannot diagnose the problem or give direction until you get specific.

Ask any parent and they will tell you emotions aren't always conveyed clearly through actions. A child may throw a tantrum for a number of reasons. Simply seeing them throw a toy and assuming they're angry is not enough. Maybe it's not anger, but loneliness, fear, or disappointment. Of course, you won't know simply by seeing their actions. You need to take the time to get under their actions and discover what's going on inside.

REMEMBER:

GET UNDER THE ACTIONS AND DISCOVER WHAT'S GOING ON INSIDE.

The same is true for each of us in every area of life: at home, in our career, and as a leader. Identifying your emotions requires going past the surface, beyond your actions, and what you can see. A trained professional can sometimes be helpful, even necessary. In my case, I needed a professional to help identify the complexity of what I was feeling during an especially significant life transition. Maybe you do, too. When we have had that help, we are better equipped to open the hood and identify the specific emotion we're experiencing in a stressful situation. (Check out the companion workbook to learn more.)

During a difficult experience, don't get so distracted by your actions that you lose sight of what's going on under the hood. And don't guess. Do the work. Dig in. And, if you need to, find someone who can help. You'll be grateful for the tools you'll receive when things break down.

FIND THE SOURCE

Knowing yourself means seeing yourself as the seat or source of your emotions. After you've opened the hood, gotten beneath the surface, and identified the particular emotion you're experiencing, the next step is identifying the source. It isn't enough to identify *what* you are feeling, you must ask *why*.

Is it a lack of sleep? Maybe, especially for a lot of young parents, how you're feeling is caused by not getting the proper rest your body needs, and it's causing you to feel out of sorts.

Or, did something happen that left you feeling let down? "Well, yeah," you might say. "I had an idea of how things were going to go, but reality didn't match that." If so, you need to ask where your expectations came from. Maybe your family or your heroes? Identifying the source of our emotion is key to understanding the reason behind that specific feeling.

I once had an employee, Tim, who didn't respond to my questions in meetings. We were a small team and his lack of response and participation made me angry. But it wasn't *really* anger. I just didn't know how to categorize what I was feeling.

As I considered the situation more, I realized Tim's lack of response *embarrassed* me. Tim's actions in this experience felt disrespectful, which was odd, because he was a very respectful person! So here I was, feeling confused by what I was feeling.

Once I pinpointed how it specifically made me feel, I could address it properly. We ended up doing personality profiles, and I understood Tim's actions weren't intentionally disrespectful— it reflected his personality type. Once we took the time to get below the surface, recognize the emotion, and name its source, we worked to improve our communication. It took effort, but the payoff was well worth it.

If you're unable to be specific with your emotions—fear, gratitude, confidence, despair, etc.—you won't be able to use them to achieve your goals. They will not be part of your toolbox for constructive thinking and problem solving. More importantly, if you do not recognize your emotions, you'll not be able to control them—they will control you. And, if you cannot recognize, let alone control, your own emotions, then you won't be able to help others recognize and control theirs.

If high EI is your aim, then take the time to learn the tools that will help you drill down into the specific emotion you're experiencing *when* you're experiencing it (for more on this, check out the companion workbook). The dividends will be huge—for yourself and for your relationships with others. EI starts with knowing yourself.

APPLYING YOUR EI

- In your own words, how would you define Emotional Intelligence? Being able to describe EI is key to putting it into action.

- On a scale of 1 to 10, how are you at naming the emotions you're experiencing, when you're experiencing them? If this is a growth area for you, consider referring to the Plutchik Wheel of Emotions (Page 32) through-out the day. Ask yourself, "What am I feeling right now?" Be as specific as possible. The more you practice, the better you'll become.

- After you have named an emotion you're experiencing, write it down and take the time to come back to it later that day. When you have more time, dig in, get under the hood, and reflect on the source. What was its cause? Write that down. Getting into the habit of naming the source is key to developing more control.

CHAPTER 2:
SELF-CONTROL

You've probably seen slapstick comedies where a steering wheel comes off in the driver's hands. But in reality, I can think of few things more frightening than driving through a mountain pass and having the steering wheel fall off. That's an apt description of a person with low EI—trying to navigate tricky roads with a revving engine of emotion but no ability to control it. Self-control is about far more than not binging at the buffet. The mark of high EI is the ability to steer your emotions.

So, let's talk about self-control. What sets apart the world's most elite athletes from the rest of us? You might say sheer physical ability. But just as important as natural talent is discipline and self-control. The most successful athletes are those who have dedicated themselves to being disciplined at every level: from what time they go to bed at night and wake up in the morning to what they eat and drink, from how they spend their time to whom they spend their time with. Being born with the right physical gifts is critical, of course, but comparing our own day-to-day routines to the routines of elite athletes reveals just how much dedication and regulation is required to reach and maintain peak performance.

Self-control is essential to performing at the highest athletic level. The same is true of those who excel at EI. Picture this: you're at home, in the middle of a heated argument, when the phone rings. We've all been there, right? If we have high EI, we can calm ourselves down by the time we answer. In other words, we can control our emotions. According to Dr. Daniel Goleman's model of Emotional Intelligence, this is the second aspect of EI: self-regulation.

If we have a low EI, however, whatever emotion arises has the power to overwhelm us, whether it's disappointment, anger, or nervousness. For example, let's say you're in the middle of a stressful work situation when your child asks for help. If you erupt with, "Get out of here!", that's a sign of low EI. When emotions from one situation spill into another, without any control, that's a sure sign that you're in need of help. When people react like that, they often say, "I can't control myself." But that's not true—they probably wouldn't yell, "Get out of here!" to their boss. And even if they lack control in the *moment*, it's still possible to build self-control when the pressure isn't on; therefore, improving their ability to handle future high-stress moments.

You may not be running against the world's fastest sprinters in the next Summer Olympic, no matter how disciplined you are, but that doesn't mean you can't perform at the highest level of EI. It takes work and it requires self-control, but it's just as possible for you as it is for anyone else. That's what we're aiming for: controlling our emotions before they control us.

> ## REMEMBER:
>
> ## CONTROL YOUR EMOTIONS, BEFORE THEY CONTROL YOU.

DON'T GIVE AWAY CONTROL

I once heard about a young boy who couldn't control his anger. He'd act out, yell, and curse. When his parents and teachers tried to address his behavior, he'd shout, "Stop irritating me!"

His mother had an idea. Seeing that he enjoyed coloring, she bought him a canvas, easel, paints, and brushes.

He was perplexed. "Why'd you buy these for me?"

"Next time you get angry," she said, "try painting your feelings."

A few days later, she went into her son's bedroom. It was filled with disturbing paintings. She took a moment to control her own fears then asked him to explain them.

One was a picture of the kids in his class who made him feel dumb. Another painting showed the kids with the nicest clothes and phones who teased him and made him feel poor. A third was of his teacher, telling him to get his act together which made him feel incapable. The final painting was of his father, who was always telling him how well he'd done at his age, making him feel worthless.

"What do all these people have in common?" his mother asked.

"They all make me so angry!" he shouted.

"I understand they're upsetting you and contributing to your anger," she said. "But they aren't *forcing* you to be angry. You're *allowing* them control over your anger. Never let other people control you."

This mother had a high EI. And through this exercise, she was inviting her son to improve his.

After my first book was published, I frequently checked my online reviews (it's a bad habit of authors). Mostly, they were positive—sharing how my book helped them—but a few were negative. One review wasn't even about my book; it was a personal attack against me—by another author! Part of me wanted to lash back with a nasty review on *his* book but that would mean I allowed him to control me.

A person with good EI can still dislike my book but would explain their reasons and perhaps make suggestions on how I can improve. Then it's my turn to demonstrate my EI level. If it's low, I'll respond by attacking. If it's high, I'll evaluate the critique, rather than feel personally attacked. But when someone does attack me personally, like that embittered author, the healthiest option is to not engage with them. As the saying goes, "It takes more courage to walk away from a fight than to fight."

EI & PHYSIOLOGY

At times, physiology may work against your best EI intentions. If someone insults my work, I can live with that. But if someone insults my son, that's completely different! My adrenaline will start to flow, my blood pressure will rise, and my heart will race. I'll become very angry and unlikely to respond with maturity.

But if this happens, I'll (hopefully) recognize my emotions and know that I'm in no state to respond. Then I'll use physiology to my advantage by regaining control using these two "tricks" that I teach my clients:

I. TAKE A BREATH

Oxygen is a great brain cleanser. It eliminates stress so you can think clearly.

Have you ever noticed the one thing a baseball pitcher does every time before he throws a pitch? It doesn't matter if his team is ahead by 20 runs, behind by 20 runs, or if it's the bottom of the ninth, with the game tied and the bases loaded. The pitcher *always* takes a deep breath. He cleanses his brain of the tension, the stress, and the negativity of the moment. Figuratively, he's removing the cobwebs from the attic.

You can do the same thing. When you're feeling overwhelmed, pause and take a deep breath. Count your breaths, all the way to ten. As you do, let your mind follow the air as it moves through your body. This will help you slow down and gain a sense of clarity and control. Pause for power so that you can self-regulate and respond the way you choose.

REMEMBER:

WHEN YOU'RE FEELING OVERWHELMED, PAUSE FOR POWER.

---

2. TAKE A BREAK

When you feel overwhelmed by stress or surging negative emotions, take a break. Intentionally step away from whatever you're working on and choose another activity. Maybe take a walk outside, giving yourself space to think and clean air to breathe. Or maybe busy yourself with a household chore, like folding the laundry or washing the dishes.

While you're walking, doing chores, or whatever, give yourself some space and examine the feelings you're experiencing. What emotion is it? Put a name on it. Then ask, "Why am I feeling this?" What happened, specifically, that caused this emotion to come out? Does your reaction seem appropriate to the situation? Maybe it did in the moment, but with a little bit of space, it likely no longer carries the same weight it did.

When you're overwhelmed or angry, you're likely to become "flooded." This means more than being hit by a flood of emotions. On a physiological level, our amygdala will put our body into "fight, flight, or freeze." It will shut down the part of our brain responsible for reasoning. No matter how logical of a person you may think you are, when you're flooded, you are literally incapable of thinking clearly—and men are more prone to this effect than women. You cannot reason your way past being flooded. Deep breaths help, but your body needs at least twenty minutes to reset.[6]

This is a crucial aspect of EI—being able to regulate and control yourself, instead of allowing the situation to control you. When you're feeling overwhelmed, wait until you have regained self-control *before* responding. Pause, center yourself, and then respond—not the other way around.

ENVISION THE AFTERMATH

After pausing to take a breath and take a break, it's prudent and instructive to envision the aftermath of a few different responses. How many things have you said or done that you wish you could undo once you were thinking clearer? This is why it's so important to take a break and think through consequences in advance.

Imagine you've put in a lot of time on a project. You feel really good about it and expect high praise. Instead, you only receive negative feedback. How would you feel? Angry, for certain. Frustrated, perhaps. Maybe even disappointed. How should you

---

[6] https://giusisilvestri.com/blog/emotional-flooding-and-what-to-do-about-it

respond? Think through a few different options and their consequences.

You could lash out in anger and tell the person they don't know what they're talking about. But what would happen next? They'll get defensive and things will escalate. What began as a critique of your work could grow into personal attacks. Furthermore, you'll lose the opportunity to discover problems you had overlooked and the chance to improve your work. Even worse, you could do permanent damage to your working relationship with that person. I know this from experience, all because I let misplaced anger get the better of me.

"Hey Mike, can I talk to you?" asked one of my trusted employees. "I heard you're thinking about having another kid. You sure that's a good idea? You seemed happier before being a parent."

Now, I love being a parent. I mean, I absolutely *love* being a dad! The stress that he blamed on parenthood was actually due to some big "discussions" (i.e., arguments) I'd been having with my wife about possibly relocating closer to her family. All of the pressure I'd been feeling erupted out of me—and landed on him.

"I can't believe you would say that!" I glared at him until he apologized and quietly stepped away. Even when I saw him the next day, I still hadn't gotten control of myself.

"You never say that when it comes to someone's kids!" I continued. "Never, ever say anything like that!" I made sure he knew how badly he'd screwed up.

It wasn't until later, after I had calmed down and got some perspective, that I realized how rude I'd been. I took out my domestic frustrations on him. Returning to the driving metaphor, my car had been out of control and I'd run over him. I tried to apologize, but the damage was done. The relationship never returned to what it had been—all because I didn't pause to envision the aftermath.

If I had, I would have first discussed my frustration with someone I trusted or spent time journaling, allowing me to honestly express how I felt while protecting the relationship. Sometimes, we act with EI, and sometimes, we do not. This was clearly an example of me *not*. Sound familiar? Have you ever damaged or destroyed a relationship because you were out of control?

Let's imagine another response to having your wonderful project criticized: gratitude.

Gratitude sounds like a surprising way to react to criticism, but if a response to your work was hard to hear, it was likely hard to share—assuming it was coming from someone who cares. My editor, Josh Kelley, likes to remind me that "Red ink equals love" (At times, I'm not sure how much I appreciate his love...). The point is, acknowledging critique with gratitude creates room for you both to better hear and benefit from one another.

In *A Beautiful Day in the Neighborhood*, Tom Hanks portrays the children's TV show host Fred Rogers. The journalist, Lloyd Vogel, has been following Rogers, trying to get the "real" scoop on this man who always seems to be happy, filled with a deep-rooted joy and peace. In one powerful scene, the two men are in Rogers' home when Lloyd asks a pointed question about his sons.

"I can't imagine it was easy growing up with you as a father," he asks Rogers, looking for a rise.

"Until recently, my oldest never told people about me," Rogers replies. "He's very private, and that's okay. And my youngest son, he genuinely tested me. But, eventually, we found our way, and now I'm very proud of both of them. But you are right, Lloyd. It couldn't have been easy on them. Thank you. Thank you for that perspective."

"You're welcome," Lloyd says, a clear look of annoyance on his face.

"Is that not the answer you were hoping for?" Rogers asks.

Responding with gratitude, like Rogers did, will often deflate a potentially heated conversation.

Let's imagine one more potential response to criticism: curiosity. Instead of anger, and in addition to gratitude, you could simply ask for more information. "I'd like to know more—why doesn't this work for you?" you can ask. "How can I improve it?"

This approach changes the interaction from adversarial to cooperative. Even if you disagree with their feedback, starting with curiosity rather than anger will improve your relationships and your work. It will also improve your emotional wellbeing and grow your EI.

WHO'S IN THE DRIVER'S SEAT?

If you've been paying attention, you've noticed a common theme in this chapter. You, and only you, are in the driver's seat. In fact, this "car" is only built for one. No one else can grab the wheel or slam on the brakes. No one else can control your emotions, your words, or your actions but yourself. Your reactions to others are yours.

Did you internally *react* to that statement? Because emotions feel so spontaneous, it's easy to believe they are not your responsibility. Or maybe you had a parent who would yell, "You make me so angry!" This can create a false belief that you were responsible for their emotions, which taught you to blame others for your emotions. But that's merely blame shifting.

I'm not saying the other people aren't responsible for what they do to you, only that you are still responsible for how you *respond* to it. Let's say that you were clearly the first person to stop at a four way stop. The next car comes up, does a quick California stop, then proceeds through the intersection, completely ignoring your turn. They broke the law and could get pulled over. But if you were to respond by speeding into the intersection and hitting them, that would be *your* fault.

Even more important than determining fault is this truth: if we don't believe we are responsible for, or capable of, choosing our emotional response to any particular event, we'll be powerless to change. Blaming others takes away our power. But when we can say, "I chose this response," then we have the power to choose a different way—especially when we have the tools to do so.

REMEMBER:

BLAMING OTHERS TAKES AWAY OUR POWER TO CHANGE.

The aim is to get to a place of such high EI that, instead of blaming others, you can say, "This is what happened, and this is how I intentionally chose to respond."

APPLYING YOUR EI

- One of the primary ways to avoid giving away control in a stressful situation is to pause for power and take a breath. Take note of this when something gets you worked up and find a way to intentionally focus on your breathing. Count to ten if it helps. Control the pace of your breathing and notice how you feel before you respond.

- In addition, find ways to take a break. If possible, remove yourself from the stressful situation and take a walk, then return with clarity and control. Your body needs at least twenty minutes to physiologically reset from a flooded state.

- Next time you respond in a regrettable way, don't allow shame to keep you from learning from it. Imagine yourself back in that situation but responding with gratitude or curiosity instead. How would that change the results? By practicing "Envision the Aftermath" after the fact, you'll equip yourself for the future.

CHAPTER 3:
SELF-MOTIVATION

If our emotions are the engine that power us, and if self-control and self-regulation are the steering wheel and brakes, then this chapter is about the gas pedal. Sure, you can go all Spock and repress your emotions, but that's like ripping the accelerator out of your car. It might be a lot safer to never leave the driveway, but you'll never get anywhere either. Having a high EI means we not only understand what motivates us, but we are able to use our emotions to take us where we want to go.

Those with a high EI live by design. They are driven by a sense of purpose and meaning, which gives them internal motivation. These people are better equipped to respond to challenges that arise because they have a long-term sense of *where* they are going, and they know *why* they are heading there. When we live without design, we steer toward our default patterns. Without intentionality, we will get stuck in a rut with our work, finances, health, time, speech, and relationships—and ruts can't ever take you somewhere new.

Yes, some people are more self-motivated than others. But motivation, like many things, *can* be built up and developed. In this chapter, we will explore three ways to improve your motivation: Reasons, Routines, and Relationships.

FIND YOUR PASSIONS

"Find a job you enjoy doing, and you will never have to work a day in your life," Mark Twain famously said. I love that quote. It encourages us to find the passion behind what we do. That to say, passion is a key part of motivation. People are passionate about many things, and everyone's passions are different, but they are what drive us.

REMEMBER:

"FIND A JOB YOU ENJOY DOING, AND YOU WILL NEVER HAVE TO WORK A DAY IN YOUR LIFE." –*MARK TWAIN*.

I have a passion for what's best for my wife and son. I am driven to make sure they are well cared for. I also have a passion for helping others realize their potential. That's one of the things that drives me most professionally. I also have a passion for comfort, but that's one I sometimes need to fight! These are just a few of my passions, and they are likely different from yours.

So, what are you passionate about? Can you name some examples? How are they part of your everyday life? Recognizing those passions is crucial to finding your motivation, even in your weekly routines. They can be the fuel that drives you day in and day out.

Does that mean you should only do things you're excited about? Not exactly. Sometimes our passion isn't directly tied to what we do, but *why* we're doing it—or who we're doing it for. For example, I am not exactly passionate about doing dishes—it's really the opposite. But I'll still wake up early to do them because I know how much my wife will appreciate it. So, my passion isn't doing the dishes, it's loving my wife. Sometimes, doing something we don't enjoy is the best way to find what we are passionate about.

Recognizing our passion traces back to having a healthy self-awareness. You should not only be aware of your current emotions, but you should also be aware of what you like and what you don't like. And you should be intentional about using those for your motivation. Naming our personal passions and including those in our daily and weekly schedule will give us the energy and motivation when we need it most.

Following our passions is a better motivation than following the highest salary (unless the highest salary allows another passion). Not only will it bring us more joy, it will also help us do great work. Find your passions, name your passions, and plan your passions into your weekly schedule. It will make a noticeable impact on your motivation. It's also important to understand that passions can change over time. Trying out new activities is a helpful way to discover new passions and sources of motivation.

ROUTINE & NOVELTY:
EVERY FEW, DO SOMETHING NEW

To maximize our motivation, we need both routine and novelty in our life. The structure of routine can help us maintain a sense of order when things feel out of control. The novelty of new activities, on the other hand, help inspire us.

No matter what else is going on in the world, there's one thing I do (almost) every single day: make my bed. This is a relatively new routine for me. I didn't always make my bed at the start of the day, but around 7:20 each morning, I now make our bed. And I don't just tidy up the top cover and pillows. I remove the covers, pull back the top sheet, and tighten the bottom, making sure it's square. Then I replace the top sheet, pulling it back to where it should be, making sure it's lined up, then I cover it all neatly with blankets and our eight pillows—yes, *eight*. This routine helps set my day in motion. Repetition creates results.

At the same time, doing the same thing over and over again can get us into a rut. So, in addition to routines, we need novelty. Introducing new activities motivates us by giving us energy. This is why we don't work seven days a week. We need to take breaks and do something different in order to be re-energized.

Those who routinely exercise must introduce new workouts into their routine. Prior to getting married, I worked out with a guy named Jason. He was a fitness guru who had previously played college football and was involved in MMA for a while. Every couple of years, he would completely change his workout routine. For a while he was a bodybuilder, then he became completely lean. By focusing on different body goals, he kept himself interested.

If, like Jason, we don't introduce new experiences into our exercise routine, we will soon get tired of doing the same old thing. Thus, struggling to stay motivated. In short, we will burn out. But introducing a new exercise or activity can help bring us new energy, which offers newfound inspiration for our life, work, and relationships.

My wife and I recently took our son roller skating. He had never been before, and we thought he might be interested in it. We wanted to give him a chance to discover a new passion. And, while he was okay with it, he wasn't passionate about it. Not like deejaying. Seriously, my 6-year-old son is a pretty passionate DJ. The important thing is that we're always encouraging him to try something new.

Similarly, a friend of mine decided to take his son snowboarding for his fifth birthday. His son had never been before but had expressed interest in it. They drove to the nearest mountain, and he rented a snowboard. His son loved it! At the end of an exhausting day, he still didn't want to stop. He was already making plans to go again and conquer "the big hill." This is an example of trying something new and discovering a new passion—an activity that brings energy, inspiration, and… motivation!

One helpful rule for me is, "For every few, do something new." For every few routine experiences, introduce something new to energize and inspire yourself.

> # REMEMBER:
>
> # FOR EVERY FEW, DO SOMETHING NEW.

Some people are naturally drawn to routine, while others are drawn to novelty. Personally, I'm attracted to new things. I have to purposefully create routines in my life, including my workday, otherwise I can bounce from different things to different things. The truth is, we need both routine and novelty. Repetition and creativity go hand-in-hand.

Having a healthy balance of routine and novelty can create a rhythm that will help you get into the groove. My niece recently introduced me to a new craze on the video sharing site, TikTok: sea shanties. That's right, sea shanties. These videos have become incredibly popular at the time I am writing this book. People are writing their own sea shanties and then recording themselves singing them all over the place.

Originally, sea shanties were created as a source of motivation for the crews on long, tedious journeys across the seas. The officers realized that, if they could get the crew singing together, they'd get in a groove and work better. This was especially true of work that required teamwork, like rowing or pulling ropes. Not only did the sea shanties help the crews avoid boredom and psychological burnout, but they also helped build camaraderie. They found a way to add novelty to their routine.

While we may not be setting out to sea, the same idea can also apply to us—whether we're working on a long project and struggling to find motivation or we're in a rut and every day feels the same. Having a rhythm of routine and new experiences can help us get in a productive groove. A healthy rhythm that balances routine and novelty will encourage you to stay motivated and improve your work and wellbeing.

RELATIONSHIPS:
COMPETITION, ACCOUNTABILITY, AND ENCOURAGEMENT

Another important factor in our motivation is relationships. Even if most of our work is done on our own, our interactions with others will motivate us. This happens primarily in three ways: relationships of *competition*, *accountability*, and *encouragement*.

My sister called me recently to let me know that she had a major breakthrough in her work as a real estate agent. After over a year of feeling like she wasn't making any progress, her business exploded. My first thought was, *Better up my game!* Having a successful sibling has been an incredible source of motivation for me since a young age. It's been unhealthy at times, and our parents occasionally had to rein it in, but I know that much of my success comes from that *relationship of competition*.

Likewise, in the workplace we are always aware of those who are coming in early or staying later than us. We push ourselves to follow suit and make sure we're putting in the time required to excel in our work. Seeing others go to extra lengths pushes us to do the same. When I was a hiring manager, I would always try to hire in pairs. I noticed that there is a healthy motivation when people measure their own performance against someone who started at the same time. This motivation not only encourages them to challenge each other, but themselves as well. So long as they don't become unhealthy, relationships of competition can be an important source of motivation.

Another relational source of motivation are *relationships of accountability*. I meet with a men's group twice a month. We spend our time catching up, sharing life stories, and barbecuing. We also commit to reading a book together and discussing it. This has been another important source of motivation in my life. I don't want to show up at the monthly meeting and be the one who hasn't done the reading. I'd feel like I'd let these guys down and wouldn't be able to enjoy myself nearly as much as if I had kept up. These friendships of accountability help me do more than I'd do on my own.

REMEMBER:

FRIENDSHIPS OF ACCOUNTABILITY DRIVE ME HARDER THAN I CAN DRIVE MYSELF.

Likewise, if we are wanting to commit to regular exercise but we struggle to get out of bed for our morning run or show up at the gym at the end of a long workday, we could benefit from having a running group or a workout partner.

This was true for one of my friends. He wanted to get into running but, between his full-time work and a young family, he'd let week after week go by without lacing up. Frustrated, he approached a friend at church who was training for a marathon and asked to join him. That may sound extreme but knowing that someone would be waiting on the corner for him in running shoes helped my friend stop making excuses and get the exercise that he needed and wanted. Years later, they still run together. Whether it's reading, exercise, or intentionally increasing your emotional intelligence, having someone hold you accountable will be a great motivation.

Lastly, *relationships of encouragement* help us stay motivated when we feel tired, down, or ready to give up. From time to time, a long-time mentor named Chad calls me up. It's not about competition. It's not about holding me accountable. He just wanted to check in and encourage me. And it makes a real difference in my life.

Relationships of encouragement are especially important when we're facing an intimidating challenge. I'm an executive coach and communications consultant, which means that I get to help people achieve their goals. One time, I was working with someone who was preparing for a huge TEDx Talk. I helped him with his delivery and stage presence, but an equally important role was to encourage him—to remind him that he was more than equal to the task.

Relationships of encouragement become essential when we are going through the inevitable rough patches. For example, a relationship that you hoped would work out but didn't. Getting over those losses takes time and, in the absence of that relationship, we need to hear from those who know and care for us. When others check in with a phone call or a text message and offer thoughtful words of encouragement, we find ourselves strengthened in ways we couldn't achieve on our own.

Another rough patch might be a job loss. Spending day after day applying for a new position is exhausting—especially when we hear that the positions went to someone else—yet we have to keep pressing ahead. This is grueling which is why we need people to check in. It is encouraging when people not only ask how we're doing but offer us reminders of our past success and good qualities. Without that, we can very easily feel like giving up. But, if we have people who are coming alongside and encouraging us, we are more likely to keep pressing ahead— sending out strong applications, being confident in ourselves when we interview, and being ready to contribute when the right opportunity comes along.

On a more personal note, some friends of mine, Tim and Kim, were struggling with infertility for years. They had spent years (and loads of money) seeking help as they watched their friends have children of their own and celebrate their growing families. With each birth announcement and birthday invitation, they felt like their hopes for children would never be fulfilled. It helped immensely that they had friends who were intimately familiar with their hopes and disappointments, and the financial and emotional costs of this experience.

But this is not only their story, because we were the friends who were also struggling with infertility. We have been incredibly grateful to have friends who could encourage us, just as we encouraged them. When we met and found out that we were going through this same struggle, we were grateful—grateful for this other couple who also shared our experiences. We began going out to Taco Tuesdays together, sharing stories and supporting one another. After years of trying to get pregnant without any success, one night over dinner, we shared that we had good news. Then, we asked Tim and Kim if they would be the godparents to our son. Three months later, they told us they were pregnant, too!

Relationships of competition, accountability, and encouragement are important sources of motivation for all of us. But when we know ourselves well, we will understand that some are more helpful than others. For example, I am naturally competitive, and I know that I am more likely to be motivated by healthy relationships of competition with my family, friends, and business associates than other sources of motivation. That doesn't mean I only have competitive relationships. But it does mean that I know these relationships will have the biggest impact on my motivation.

> ### REMEMBER:
>
> ## WHEN WE KNOW OURSELVES, WE KNOW WHAT MOTIVATES US—CAPITALIZE ON THAT KNOWLEDGE.

How about you? What relationships are most impactful on your motivation? Do you respond best to healthy competition, accountability, or encouragement? If you're feeling un-motivated, is it because one of these is lacking? Using these categories will help you discover and leverage your most effective sources of motivation.

APPLYING YOUR EI

- What life passions would you like to explore more in your life? Write down one or two that feel untapped. What are some practical ways you can introduce opportunities to explore those? Notice how exploring them encourages motivation in other areas of life.

- What comes more naturally to you: routine or novelty? Which of these is more challenging? Notice where you would like to grow—maybe it's establishing an exercise routine for each week. Or, maybe it's introducing new activities into your established schedule, like going for a hike to celebrate the end of the week, or volunteering in your community. Either way, commit to doing "something new every few" in the next week. Notice how this balance of routine and novelty will inspire and energize you.

- Relationships of *competition*, *accountability*, and *encouragement* are essential to staying motivated. Which of these three types of relationships are most effective for you? Which is currently lacking in your life? Do you know anyone who is a model of that particular relationship? In the next months, find time to speak with them about creating stronger relationships in this area.

PART II: **THEM**

CHAPTER 4:
IDENTIFYING

Have you ever been driving along the highway and just *knew* what a car was about to do, like change lanes without signaling? It's hard to explain, but after driving for so many years, you've developed the ability to read traffic. You may not always be right, but you're right more often than not.

I've been comparing EI to going on a road trip with friends. Once you've got a good handle on your own "car," you have to get on the road and interact with "them"—the other people that may or may not have a good handle on their own cars. Part Two is about understanding and connecting with those other cars—first, by identifying their feelings, then by empathizing with them, and finally, by engaging with them.

––––––––––––––

READING THE ROOM

When I arrive at a venue for a speaking gig, the first thing I do is check out the stage and make sure the equipment is working. Then, I do a little reading. But I don't read a book or my notes. I read the room. Standing off to the side, I look at the faces in my soon-to-be-audience. I read their body language.

Does the audience look like they are in a good mood? Are they smiling? Or do they look like they would rather be at their dentist's office, undergoing a root canal? Do they look like they want to hear from me or are they being forced into the room by their boss? Identifying my audience's emotions before I begin speaking helps me to ensure a connection when I begin. And connecting with others is one of the most important things we can do.

Relationships are essential to a meaningful life, and they affect every aspect of it. Connecting well with others improves our health, our work, and others' wellbeing. Those who cannot connect well with others often struggle in life. In many ways, connecting is at the heart of everything in this book. Ultimately, leadership is nothing more and nothing less than connection.

While some people are natural-born connectors, we can all improve. Being able to connect well requires three actions: Identifying, Empathizing, and Engaging. Over the next three chapters, we'll walk through each of these actions together, starting with identifying others' emotions.

NONVERBAL COMMUNICATION

Research suggests that as much as 90 percent of communication is nonverbal. Rather than putting their emotions into words, people often express how they feel with facial expressions, tone of voice, hand gestures, body movements, and more. Emotions are not as private as we might think. We are routinely putting them on display, and we can read them in others, if we know what to look for.

REMEMBER:

AS MUCH AS 90 PERCENT OF COMMUNICATION IS NONVERBAL.

We all noticed the importance of nonverbal communication when people began wearing face masks during the COVID-19 pandemic, didn't we? You'd ask the cashier how they were doing and maybe they didn't pick up on your question because they couldn't see your mouth moving. Or they had to ask, several times, "What did you say?" If we can't see one another fully, we struggle to understand just what we're communicating.

Identifying other people's emotions is essential for connecting and possessing a high EI. From a young age, those who have a hard time identifying others' emotions struggle to make friends. A school bully, for example, may misread a completely neutral expression as angry or hostile, and then lash out at another student or even a teacher. If this isn't addressed, what began as bullying at school can easily grow into workplace hostility.

In addition to misinterpreting neutral nonverbal cues as aggressive, those who struggle to identify others' emotional cues correctly aren't as likely to excel in the classroom or at work. Studies have shown that a child who has trouble reading faces will not perform to their full academic potential. Likewise, those who have trouble "reading a room" will not reach their full career potential. They also risk being passed up on jobs and promotions while their high EI peers move ahead.

Being able to pick up on and rightly identify others' emotions, including nonverbal cues, is key to creating and maintaining meaningful connections—and this begins before others ever open their mouths to speak.

There are two primary ways we can identify other people's emotions without them verbalizing what they're feeling: either we are able to "read" them, or we put ourselves in their shoes and feel what they feel. Both of these approaches are important for identifying what others are feeling. We will talk more about the second approach in the next chapter. For now, let's focus on the first approach.

People are constantly putting what they are feeling inside on display, often without them even realizing it. Our brains are hard-wired to read other people's emotions. Using imaging technology, scientists have shown that specific parts of our brains "light up" differently when we're reading other people's facial expressions than when we're looking at a picture of a mountain, for example, or a beach. As we watch their faces, our brains pick up on each movement, which will help us pair that expression with an associated emotion. This begins with watching and interpreting facial expressions, but emotions, especially more complex ones, are communicated through a combination of behaviors that goes beyond facial expressions.

Happiness, for example, typically involves a smile, but it also usually includes a cheerful tone of voice, and a relaxed posture. Anger is demonstrated by a furrowed brow or squinty eyes, but also usually includes a lower tone of voice and a constricted posture. Fear will usually appear as shifty eyes, but you can also notice that it leaves people with shortened breath (which is why some people often struggle to catch their breath when they are speaking in public). All of these physical behavior patterns help us recognize what someone else is feeling inside.

LISTEN CURIOUSLY

Ninety percent of communication is nonverbal, but that remaining 10% is absolutely crucial to understand—and that starts with really, *really* listening.

When others are speaking, what is your natural response? If you're like most people, you're likely planning what you're going to say next. Try this instead: be curious. Listen not only to *what* others are saying, the content of their communication, but *how* they're saying it, the tone of their communication.

As you begin listening curiously, can you pick up on the emotion behind their message? What they convey is so much more than just the words that they speak. Does their tone of voice suggest a joy in what they're sharing? Fatigue? Or perhaps even sadness? What about their facial expression?

As you listen to others with curiosity, notice whether their face, posture, and hand gestures match their words. If their message is that they have some exciting news to share, is that mirrored in their expression? Likewise, if it's painful news, do they look saddened? A misalignment in verbal and nonverbal messages can reveal that something deeper is going on. Picking up on this misalignment can help you identify more than what's simply being spoken. It can help you connect and ultimately address the real issue.

REMEMBER:

A MISALIGNMENT IN VERBAL AND NONVERBAL MESSAGES CAN REVEAL THAT SOMETHING MORE IS GOING ON.

Once you start looking for this misalignment, you'll notice that it happens quite often! A good portion of my week is working with high-caliber professionals, offering communication coaching. During these meetings, there have been many instances where this difference between nonverbal and verbal communication shows up. I'll share one with you.

I was once working with a regional sales manager who oversees a team of staff. He came to me to talk about his approach and shared he wasn't getting the traction that he wanted. I asked for some sample communication pieces, and we walked through those together. I played the role of one of his employees. After we had done this for a while, I asked some digging questions.

"How do you feel about your employees?"

"I like them," he said. "I like this guy, Tony. And Shandra is a rock star!"

"What is it that you want for them?" I asked.

"I really want them to do well," he said. "I want them to hit their commission, to hit their goals."

Everything he was saying about his employees was positive, which is great, but there was a problem.

"That's not what you're showing me with your face," I told him. "It's showing a lack of interest. From avoiding eye contact to not smiling, to your expressions and tone of voice—they're all saying something, but it doesn't match your words."

I lifted up some documents in front of me until they blocked the bottom half of his face and stared at them as I continued. "When you talk 'through' your notes, when you look at them instead of your staff, you might as well say to them, 'You're not worthy of my time.'"

"Wow," he said, surprised. "That's definitely not what I want to communicate!"

We had work to do. We started with adjusting his tone and his nonverbal cues, then we addressed his posture and his eye-contact. Lastly, we made sure he nodded to show he was listening. All of this helped his verbal and nonverbal communication align.

By listening with curiosity, you can identify these misalignments in others' communication and ultimately help them communicate what it is they want to share.

REVERSING OTHERS' FEELINGS

Not allowing others to control your emotions does not mean *not* helping others to control theirs (pardon the double negative). That's a totally different situation. Caring about and for other people frequently means helping them reverse—i.e. deal with and overcome—negative feelings.

How many times have you literally or figuratively held someone in your arms and reassured them that everything would be okay? The only way you could have done that, with any degree of sincerity, is if you had gone through something similar. Sure, they may have been fired and you never have been. But maybe you have suffered a death in the family, so you are familiar with the emotions surrounding loss. Tapping into that experience would allow you to respond helpfully.

Can you understand how important knowing what is under your own "hood" can be when it comes to listening to others? When I was 10 years old, my family moved to Mexico to work with a non-profit organization—it was the "tossed into the deep end of the pool" approach to learning Spanish. Because of that, I have many painful memories of being laughed at in a foreign classroom (all over the world kids are often cruel). Much of the counseling I talked about in Part One was necessitated by these childhood wounds. But by understanding my own pain, I've been able to help others deal with theirs.

We start with identifying the other person's feelings, but another important part of EI is helping this person do something about these feelings. It is about helping this person reverse unproductive and negative feelings. That can be very difficult.

A friend of mine was once working at a children's mental health center, a small center that served around 30 children. He was not a therapist; he was responsible for all non-clinical matters, from ordering supplies to payroll. The children were called the "identified patients." In other words, they were in therapy even though their parents, who were also being helped, were the real problems. In essence, the children were being taught EI so that they could deal with their parents.

One day, my friend was alone in the office when the phone rang. He answered it and was soon speaking with the mother of one of the children. Her husband was a police officer. She said that she had had enough. When her husband brought their son home from school, she said she was going to shoot them both and then herself.

Speaking with her, my friend managed to calm her down. He got her to promise to give him five minutes so he could get the coordinator to call her back. He then sprinted across the campus to where the coordinator was in a training session with the other counselors and barged in. Of course, they were all trained in EI and recognized his emotions. He was completely out of breath, but they could tell he was scared and something was very wrong.

He caught his breath. "Call, call Kyle's mom! She's...she's gonna kill...son...dad...self!"

The coordinator jumped up and ran out of the room. One of the therapists gave my friend his chair and some water. Everyone started asking what he'd said to the mother.

"I...I can't remember!" my friend said in panic.

"It's okay," said a psychologist. "That's normal. You're doing great..."

Remember, my friend was in charge of non-clinical operations. He didn't know the complexities of psychology and mental health. He could have easily made matters worse, and he knew it. But they helped him calm himself down.

A few minutes later, the program coordinator returned to the room after having spoken with the mother. She, too, asked my friend what he had said to the mother. He still could not remember.

"Well, the mom said you were great," she told him. "And she wants you to be the family's therapist!"

As my friend was leaving, the psychologist congratulated him on a job well done but also wanted him to understand something: a person in therapy can proclaim that life is good one day. Maybe they have just gotten a new job. They have registered for a new class or a program. Or maybe they have a new love interest. And then, that same evening, they can go home and take their own life.

On the other hand, someone can say that life is terrible. They can explain that they are going to be fired. That their significant other is going to dump them. Or that their parents are nagging them relentlessly, and they cannot escape judgment. They can explain that their life is a series of disappointments, and they feel they no longer have any reason to live. And that person, unlike the other patient who insisted that life is good, that person will die of natural causes at a ripe old age.

Here's the lesson: you cannot always tell what a person is really, truly feeling. They may be hiding their emotions. In fact, don't feel bad if you misread someone's emotional state. They may not only be lying to you, they may be lying to themselves. But if you are self-aware, and if you can identify other people's emotions, you're more than halfway there to helping them— especially when you have the EI to know what to do.

REMEMBER:

IT IS NOT YOUR *RESPONSIBILITY* TO IDENTIFY OTHER PEOPLE'S EMOTIONS, BUT IT IS SMART TO DO SO.

It is not your *responsibility* to identify other people's emotions, but it is smart to do so. Taking the time to identify what others are feeling—for example, by listening with curiosity or by using the Emotional Wheel—is the first step in connecting with others. The next step involves moving beyond identifying to actually experiencing what they are feeling.

APPLYING YOUR EI

- When you're speaking with people this week, pay special attention to their nonverbal communication. Facial expressions, hand gestures, and posture will help you identify what they're feeling. Afterward, take a minute to write down what you noticed, without referring to their words, and what that tells you about your interaction.

- This week, when other people are talking, make a special effort to lean in with curiosity. Whenever you notice that you're thinking about what you're going to say next, intentionally focus your attention back to them.

- When you're listening to other people speak this week, pay attention to any misalignment between verbal and nonverbal communication. If appropriate, help them explore that by asking a nonjudgmental question or comment, such as, "You don't *seem* to be as happy as you say you are."

CHAPTER 5:
EMPATHIZING

It's one thing to understand the other "cars" on the road—to read what they are doing and respond accordingly. It is another to see those cars as *people*. You've probably heard the expression "The Good Samaritan." It comes from a story Jesus told his followers. In that parable, the respected religious leaders ignored a badly wounded person and treated him as an inconvenience. It was only the Samaritan who saw him as a person. That is the challenge of this chapter—learning to see others as people with thoughts, feelings, and needs that are just as important as our own.

In the run up to the 2016 U.S. Presidential election, immigration was one of the hottest issues. This was not an abstract topic where I was living, a semi-rural agricultural area about an hour north of Seattle with a large immigrant population.

A decade before I lived there, there was a spike in gang violence. Some of the gang members included second and third-generation immigrants. Because of this, I could see how some members of that community were wary of immigration. And so, in 2016, this conversation became very heated, not just nationally, but locally. "Immigrants are taking our jobs," some were saying. "Immigrants are causing crime," others suggested.

On the other side, people were pointing out that immigrants were looking for safety, and a place to work—which are basic concerns for all of us, no matter where we're from.

Likewise, this wasn't just a political or ideological conversation for me. I have friends who are personally affected. One of those friends was a young man in his early thirties, a great guy whose parents brought him to the U.S. when he was just four years old. He came to me, looking very anxious and upset.

"Mike, I'm terrified," he said. "If the Dreamer policy goes away, I'm afraid that I might be deported—I haven't lived in Mexico since I was four!"

Additionally, growing up in Mexico has left a lasting mark on my life, including life-long friendships. Many of those friends are still an important part of my life today. And, having lived in Mexico for years, I know that it was common for fathers to live away much of the year, sharing a small apartment with several other men and working to send money back to their family. They weren't present for their children, but they were able to provide.

One benefit that these international friendships have offered me is that immigration isn't just an abstract conversation; these are people I know. So, when I hear it being discussed, either in-person or in the media, it's far more than an academic debate. This is a conversation that directly affects my friends. Knowing other people's experience with immigration has changed how I talk about it because I know something of their experience.

> # REMEMBER:
>
> ## EMPATHY IS THE CENTER AND CENTRAL POINT OF EMOTIONAL INTELLIGENCE.

If we're going to connect with others, we must move beyond just identifying what they are feeling. We must truly understand their perspective. We must empathize with them. Empathy is the center and central point of EI.

THE BENEFITS OF EMPATHY

The word empathy comes from two Greek words: *en*, meaning "in," and *pathos*, or "feeling." Empathy and sympathy are often confused. Sympathy involves feeling concern for others. Empathy, however, involves actually feeling what others are experiencing. It means feeling *with*.

When we can feel what others feel, we are able to show them that they are heard, which is a helpful way to create positive connections. And, when we can empathize with others, we will benefit in many other areas of our own life.

Research shows that those who excel at empathy are more likely to be emotionally healthy. They are more popular, do better in school (even if their IQ is not higher), and are more likely to have meaningful romantic relationships. Those who are married know that being high in empathy can dramatically improve your connection.

REMEMBER:

THOSE WHO EXCEL AT EMPATHY ARE MORE LIKELY TO BE EMOTIONALLY HEALTHY, BE MORE POPULAR, DO BETTER IN SCHOOL, AND HAVE MORE MEANINGFUL RELATIONSHIPS.

Others are beginning to note the way that empathy drastically improves their work. Teachers who are able to pick up on their students' feelings are more likely to teach them in helpful and effective ways than those who struggle to recognize what their students need or want. Salespeople and managers have long known that empathy creates meaningful connections in their work and makes the difference between success and failure. Leaders who can empathize with their employees will be better suited to motivate their staff in effective ways. They will be more likely to connect with them and will be better at responding to challenges.

One line of work where empathy's importance is increasingly being recognized is law enforcement. At a time when police officers across the country are being monitored more and more closely, some are suggesting that empathy is the key to successful policing, without resorting to violence. Exercises that increase empathy are now being introduced in police training across the country. An officer in Washington State, interviewed by *The New Yorker*, notes that empathy is changing how they do their work, for the better.

"It's a safety strategy that gives officers a tactical advantage. When you know why someone is acting a certain way, you also know how to best react." [7]

EMPATHETICALLY CHALLENGED

In contrast, those who struggle to empathize are more likely to struggle in life. Not just relationally, but in other areas driven by their inability to see other people as people.

For example, take those who engage in criminal behavior. Some have suggested that rapists, child molesters, and sociopaths are actually incapable of empathy. However, recent research suggests that when sociopaths behave without empathy it's not because they are unable to empathize with others, but because they fail to use empathy automatically. [8] In fact, they're actively working to stop or manipulate it.

This prolonged blotting out of their empathy leads to them to no longer feel what others are feeling. Becoming so calloused

---

[7] *The New Yorker*, "When Cops Choose Empathy," September 25, 2015: https://www.newyorker.com/tech/annals-of-technology/when-cops-choose-empathy.

[8] *Science Daily*, July 24, 2013: https://www.sciencedaily.com/releases/2013/07/130724200412.htm, accessed March 30, 2021.

allows these criminals to treat others with horrific cruelty. The good news is that, even in those who have intentionally diminished their ability to empathize with others, empathy can be repaired, restored, and even developed through intentional practice and therapy.

It's easy to dismiss those previous examples since you're probably not a hardened criminal. Sociopaths' defective empathy may be self-imposed, but there are other challenges to empathy that occur "naturally." Research has shown that in situations of conflict between opposing groups, our ability to empathize breaks down. In racial or political conflict, for example, we struggle to empathize as much with those from an outside group as we would with those within our own group. In a 2009 study in Britain, researchers found that students responded more empathetically to news of the death of a student's parent if they were told that that student was from their own school instead of an opposing school. In these cases, something is getting in the way of our ability to feel what others feel—namely, group divisions.

Unfortunately, being empathetically challenged is practically our default mode. The classic leadership book *Leadership and Self-Deception: Getting out of the Box*, is all about our tendency to treat others as problems instead of people (If you haven't read it, you need to check it out). Even with the best of motives, empathy is hard to maintain. For instance, when we're overwhelmed or stressed, we are unable to process information as we normally would, leaving our emotions and decision-making faculties hard-pressed. In marital conflict, for example, when our emotions are flooded, we often struggle to hear our spouse in non-defensive ways, let alone allow ourselves to feel what they're feeling. This is especially true for those who are experiencing chronic anxiety, either because of their work, relationships, or living conditions. When stress is constantly running high, we no longer have the mental and emotional bandwidth needed to feel what others are feeling, to make rational judgements, and to respond with high EI.

IMPROVING YOUR EMPATHY

The point of all of this is that empathy is central to Emotional Intelligence. In fact, psychologist Dr. Goleman refers to empathy as "the fundamental people skill." Without empathy, your EI will always be low—end of story.

REMEMBER:

EMPATHY IS THE FUNDAMENTAL PEOPLE SKILL.

So how do we fix low empathy? Generally speaking, women are better than men at empathy. No surprise there, right? And some children are better at empathy than others, especially those in homes where their wellbeing requires being aware of their parents' emotions. Regardless of whether empathy comes naturally or not, and regardless of the particular challenges to empathy that you're experiencing, research shows that *empathy is something we can all improve in*. Empathy is less of a fixed trait and more of a learned skill.

But it takes effort.

REMEMBER:

EMPATHY IS LESS OF A FIXED TRAIT AND MORE OF A LEARNED SKILL.

EXPLORE THEIR PERSPECTIVE

Something as simple as reading a novel can improve our ability to empathize, helping us to feel what it's like to experience someone else's perspective. One of my favorite books is *Les Miserables* by Victor Hugo, and empathy is one of its central themes.

The main character is Jean Valjean. Shaped by his own experience of nearly 20 years of imprisonment, after stealing bread to feed his family, Jean Valjean is shown mercy at a pivotal point in his life. Following this experience of mercy, Valjean is repeatedly seen acting on behalf of others in need. After he has found political and professional success as a mayor and the owner of a factory, Valjean takes in the child of one of his workers, Cosette, saving her from a life of poverty and so many other life-threatening dangers. In his care, Cosette flourishes.

Valjean's own experience with hardship and grace allows him to feel others' experience of pain and respond with compassion and support. It's impossible to read (or watch) this story and not be moved by it!

Another way to improve our empathy is by spending time with people who are different from us and who can provide first-hand access to a perspective different from our own. The trouble is, this requires intentional effort.

A powerful example of the effort required to empathize with others comes from the 2016 Presidential Election. Without getting partisan, I was really impressed with one journalist's response when Donald Trump won the United States Presidential Election. This reporter could not fathom how someone could have voted for Donald Trump, regardless of their political position, and, as a result, she couldn't understand how he won. Rather than blast those who voted for him, calling them names or ridiculing them like so many others had, she tried to sincerely understand their perspective. "Help me understand what I am not seeing" became her posture. This meant actually visiting those who voted for Trump, spending time together, and, most importantly, listening without judgment.

She visited three different families and discovered something that went well beyond political affiliation or partisan reasons. For instance, she traveled all the way to Alaska and found out that one of the Obama Administration regulations that she was in favor of had a very significant and negative impact on their economy. "It didn't change my view," she shared afterward, "but it changed my perspective."

Her own personal political position did not change, but her perspective on other people did. It was only by taking the time to listen without judgement that she was able to understand why they voted as they did. This is an example of the kind of effort required to truly get to know someone else's perspective, which is key to empathy.

WALK IN THEIR SHOES

Not all of us can hop on a flight to Alaska in order to understand someone else's perspective, but we can all make the effort to walk in someone else's shoes. One of the biggest mistakes we can make when connecting with others is judging how others speak or act based on our own experience, rather than trying to understand and feel theirs. Correcting this mistake can go a long way in helping us to create meaningful connections, especially with those whose perspective is different from our own.

Anne was one of my interns. She was performing in a lackluster way, so I was getting ready to write her a very difficult email. I was going to let her have it! That was my first response, but with all that I'd learned about EI, I decided to delete the email and go to her. "Anne, what's going on in your life?" I asked.

I found out that the shoes Anne was walking in were very uncomfortable—her personal life was filled with challenges I hadn't known about. I was so glad I hadn't sent that email and made it worse! By taking the time to experience what she was experiencing, I was able to give her the grace and direction that she needed. She still had to "course correct," but my new understanding allowed me to help her do so without adding to her burden.

New York psychologist Dr. Martin Hoffman has made a career out of researching empathy. Dr. Hoffman's work has focused on the development of empathy and its relationship to morality. According to his findings, empathizing with others leads us to act on their behalf. When we are able to walk in others' shoes, we're more likely to offer help. Empathy encourages us to be the kind of people we all aspire to be. Hoffman's research also found that those who empathize with others and act on their behalf reported feeling better when they do. Empathy is good for our health!

At the same time, getting close enough to others to truly walk in their shoes can be intimidating, scary, or even feel wrong. The riots that broke out across the U.S. in 2020 were enough to unnerve any of us. Watching videos of buildings being destroyed, cars being set on fire, and police in riot gear fending off crowds was deeply unsettling, especially while we were already feeling the disorienting experience of the COVID-19 pandemic. However, rather than merely acting with judgement and alarm, it is worth asking *why* so many chose to respond in this way. Right or wrong, what feelings and experiences were fueling the need to destroy public property or the property of small business owners? If we take the time to listen and imagine ourselves in others' situations, we are more likely to be able to empathize—even if we don't respond in the same way.

A St. Louis pastor shared about choosing to participate in peaceful demonstrations for the first time. This pastor had never felt compelled to participate before, though he knew many who did. But that all changed when he heard a story from a young mother in his congregation. She shares about the time she watched tear gas seep into her apartment and how she was doing her best to keep her children safe from its toxic effects. After hearing that experience, this pastor was affected. He imagined himself in her shoes, trying to keep his own children safe in his home and that led him to act. He began leading peaceful demonstrations in his community, creating opportunities for conversation with local law enforcement leaders and elected officials. Allowing himself to feel what this young mother felt affected not only his emotions, but his actions.

There is a direct correlation between empathy and caring for others. Allowing yourself to feel what others are feeling is a crucial way to grow your empathy, to encourage care for others, and to create connective bridges.

APPLYING YOUR EI

- In conversations this week, notice when you're sympathizing and when you're empathizing. Work on moving past simply identifying what others are feeling and make an intentional effort to feel what others are feeling. How does this change your interaction?

- What is one way that you can explore the perspective of someone who thinks differently than you this week? Try getting your news from "the other side's" outlet. Rather than simply jumping to judgment, ask, "Why are they saying that?" "What is leading them to that perspective?" This takes work but exploring others' perspectives will help improve your empathy—even if you still disagree.

- This week, try to put yourself in someone else's shoes— someone whose experience is very different from your own. Maybe it's a family member, a colleague, or the homeless man you pass by on your daily commute. Whoever it is, spend five to ten minutes imagining what their day was like. Afterward, write down what emotions you felt as you did. Commit to exploring this practice with a different person each week for the entire month.

- _____

- _____

- _____

- _____

- _____

- _____

- _____

CHAPTER 6:
ENGAGING

We've all been there. Traffic is crawling along, and your exit is coming up. You turn on your blinker and hope for the best. The car to your right shows mercy and lets you merge. You slide in and give them a quick "thank you" wave. Without a word, you have connected with them.

There's more to EI than identifying what others are feeling and empathizing with them. You need to engage with them, to connect on some level. Some time ago, I discovered the ALAER process to help me effectively engage with others, using the steps: Ask, Listen, Acknowledge, Explore, and Respond.

I like to refer to this process as flying a kite. Like flying a kite, it involves repeatedly checking in and renegotiating. If you simply let out a little string and hope to fly, you're going to be disappointed. Things are soon going to come to an abrupt end—as my son has found out! Similarly, if you're looking to connect with others and you simply ask a question and stop, you're going to be sorely disappointed. In both cases, you need to do more to gain traction and keep things going. When you're flying a kite, you need to regularly check the connection with the line and the same is true in connecting with others, using the ALAER approach.

As we walk through each of these steps, you'll see how they build on everything we've learned so far.

ASK QUESTIONS

The first step in the ALAER approach is asking questions. Asking questions helps to create conversation. Sometimes they are as simple as, "How has your week been going?" Or, if you're already connected, they can be more specific.

REMEMBER:

THOUGHTFUL QUESTIONS SHOW GENUINE INTEREST.

For example, let's say you're chatting with a doctor about their approach to vaccinating patients. After hearing a brief overview of how they are offering their patients a choice in what vaccine they receive, you may say something like, "Can you tell me a little bit more about why patients' freedom of choice is important to you?" Taking the time to ask thoughtful questions shows you're genuinely interested in learning more.

LISTEN ACTIVELY

The next step in connecting through the ALAER approach is "Listening Actively." This means not just waiting for others to finish so that you can respond. Instead, show the other person that you're really hearing what is being said by using your nonverbal cues. While the other person is speaking, make sure that you're maintaining eye contact, showing interest with both your facial expressions and your body posture. Also, ensure that you're not distracted, either by anything else going on nearby or your own thoughts. This not only helps you really hear them, but it demonstrates to them that they are being heard, which opens them up to share more.

ACKNOWLEDGE THE HEART

The next step involves speaking up to acknowledge the heart of what has just been said. When the other person has finished speaking, without interrupting them, pause for a second or two to make sure they are really done, then acknowledge what was said with a statement like, "I hear you saying… Did I get that right?" Then, acknowledge how the other person feels. You can say, "That must have made you feel frustrated." Or, "I can imagine you were celebrating after that!" Check to make sure that what you're describing is accurate—look for a nod or some sort of agreement—before continuing.

Next, show that you understand *why* they feel that way. You can say something like, "If that would have happened to me, I would have felt the same." Or share an example of a similar experience from your own life. But if you do share one of your own experiences, keep it short and intentionally bring it back to what the other person has shared. This will help avoid shifting the focus to yourself.

EXPLORE CURIOUSLY

After you have actively listened to them and acknowledged the heart of what has been shared, take time to explore more with them before you respond. Even after you have asked an initial question, dig deeper into what has been said so that you can gain even more understanding. This step is likely to feel the least natural, so it is helpful to reflect on it and take the time to practice.

Let's return to the example of the doctor speaking about vaccines. After they have shared a bit more about why patient choice is so important to them, you might explore this further by asking what would happen if this *weren't* their commitment. "What kind of a patient would that create?" you might ask. And, "Why does that matter to you, as a physician?"

Asking exploratory questions based on what has been shared after listening actively shows that you've understood, and that you're interested in learning more. One word of caution: be careful not to over-pry in this step. The point is to show interest and expand your understanding, not to pry.

RESPOND APPROPRIATELY

Only after you have done this several times, when you have a full picture of the other person's situation and experience, should you finally respond with your own perspective or offer a suggestion. When you have done this several times *before* responding, you'll avoid the mistake of *assuming* you know what they need. Instead, you'll be able to speak into what the other person *actually* needs.

Here's another example of an ALAER approach to connecting. You're speaking with Alex (in bold), who is having a difficult time at work, and you're using the ALAER approach (non-bold). The letters identify which part of the ALAER process you are engaging in at that point:

A: Ask questions

L: Listen actively

AH: Acknowledge the Heart

E: Explore

R: Respond

Here's the conversation with Alex:

A   "Alex! How's it going?"

L   **"Meh. Just the same thing, again and again."**

AH   "I hear you. I have felt that way, too."

E   "What are you referring to specifically? The monotony of Zoom and virtual work, or something else?"

L   **"Sure, the same old calls are part of it. But I've gotten used to that—most days. I mean how they communicate with us on projects. Halfway done, and *Boom*! they want us to change everything. Total waste. Why do anything until I know what they actually want?"**

AH   "Sounds like you're having to redo your work because 'they' keep changing it? Must be frustrating."

L   **"It is, yeah."**

E   "Who are 'they'?"

L   **"Supposedly the CEO, but I have a feeling it's my boss, like he's trying to cover his backside."**

AH   "Shoot. That sounds really challenging. I'm sorry you're in this tough spot."

———————

This conversation could go back and forth like this for a while. Eventually, the Exploration leads to a Response. Sometimes the Response is simply empathy:

R   "I understand. I'm with you."

Other times it involves offering to help. Another response to Alex's situation could sound something like this:

R "You know what, Alex? Let me talk to your manager and see what's going on."

Still another response could be to suggest that the other person take an active step in addressing the issue:

R "You might want to set up a meeting with your manager. You know, explain how these changes are making it difficult to be effective. Maybe the two of you can create a better system for work requests."

Here's another example of the ALAER approach (without labels), this time from my own experience dealing with concerned staff members. I once had an employee, Nathan, who came to me one day and blurted out: "We have to do something! *Everyone* is angry."

"Oh no…Tell me more," I said, inviting more of an explanation.

"Well," Nathan began, "when we changed the schedule, everyone got really upset!"

"Oh," I said, taking a pause. "Was it the changes, specifically, that were upsetting, or something else?"

"It was definitely the changes to the schedule," Nathan said. "That much is clear."

"Oh, okay. And you said everybody is upset about it. Who is everybody?"

"*Everybody,*" Nathan insisted.

"Wow. That's a lot of people," I said. "Can you give me some names?"

"Okay. Mark. And Sandy…"

"Mark and Sandy?" I asked.

"Yes."

"So, two people?" I clarified.

"Yeah."

"Okay. Well, don't worry anymore about it—I'll follow up with them and take care of this. Okay?"

"Okay," Nathan said. "Thanks!"

Nathan left relieved, confident that he had been heard, and that the situation was going to be addressed. He was now able to return to his work and focus on what he needed to do with a peace of mind. And I now had a clear path on how to follow up to address the issue, and who to follow up with.

The point of the ALAER approach is to not just simply understand what others are sharing. It is to help others understand *that* you understand. Taking the time to walk through each of these steps—Asking questions, Listening actively, Acknowledging the heart, Exploring curiously, and then Responding appropriately—will help you build a bridge to connect with, and relate to, others.

> ## REMEMBER:
>
> ## ALAER HELPS YOU UNDERSTAND—
> ## AND HELPS THEM KNOW THAT
> ## YOU UNDERSTAND.

APPLYING YOUR EI

- Which of the steps in the ALAER approach seems most natural to you? What is one takeaway from this chapter that will help you get even better at that one?

- What step seems most unnatural or difficult for you? What is one way you can improve with that particular step this week?

- Flying a kite with the ALAER approach can be helpful for connecting with others in a variety of relationships, from an emotionally distant family member to a challenging work relationship. Name one relationship where this could help you create a deeper connection and commit to putting it into practice this week.

PART III: US

CHAPTER 7:
CONNECTING

You've got your car under control, you're working with the other cars on the highway, but now you've got to work together with all your friends in their own cars so you can caravan to your destination together. You glance down at your phone to read the text thread (Shame on you—eyes on the road!). One friend just sent a cat gif, another says they need to use the bathroom and wants to get off on the next exit. The "alpha" of the group (is that you?) says they should just hold it. Yeah, everyone is working towards the same objective, but there might be some bumps in the road.

How do you feel about work parties? Or group projects? Or, for those who attend church, that moment when your pastor asks you to greet those around you? Some of us are confident in these social settings. We love meeting and getting to know new people. We love opportunities to collaborate. For others, these same situations can make us panic.

When it comes to connecting and engaging with others, we are talking about situations that involve social skills. More important to your professional advancement than any technical skills are the social skills that help you navigate social settings with confidence and ease. The good news is that, no matter how anxious you feel in social situations, these skills can be learned, developed, and improved.

In Part Three, we're going to build on everything we've learned so far. Part One was about "me" and Part Two was about "them"—those we interact with daily. Part Three is about "us" and will cover three different aspects of relationships: Meeting, Maintaining, and Solving.

To begin, we're going to cover the five different levels of friendship. Everyone in the entire world can be put into one of these five categories. Next, we will cover the social skills that will remove the anxiety from meeting new people, allowing you to thrive and effectively connect. Every social interaction involves a multitude of unwritten and written rules. Those who have a high EI know how to navigate these expectations in a way that puts others at ease, creates positive interactions, and grows deeper connections.

Then, we will cover the different communication styles at play in our interactions with one another—Aggressive, Passive, Passive-Aggressive, and Assertive—and identify ways to best navigate these different communication styles. And, lastly, we'll cover how you can most effectively use assertive communication to connect with others.

FIVE LEVELS OF FRIENDSHIP

Every friendship starts somewhere. Think about it—in all your friendships, there was a point when that friend was once a stranger. That's the starting point for any relationship, and the *first level* of friendship. A stranger is someone with whom you co-exist with. You don't know their name, and they don't know yours. Meeting for the first time is the start of a relationship, and that first meeting is where you move from being a stranger to increasingly deeper levels of friendship.

The *second level* of friendship is an acquaintance. An acquaintance is someone you share space and some sort of an activity with. Maybe your kids are on the same soccer team. Or you're in the same workspace. You're acquainted with them, you *might* know their name, and you know something about them.

The *third level* is a casual friend. This is the type of person you recognize and have spent time with. You share something in common with them. Maybe you've had a meal or played racquetball together, likely with others. Closer than just an acquaintance, seeing this person brings a smile to your face. However, casual friends are likely to keep the conversation in the positive realm, sharing successes and wins. But casual friendships don't really move beyond that. If you were to relocate to a new city tomorrow, it's unlikely this relationship will continue. By the way, studies show that most of your new professional connections will come from this level. Surprised? The reason is that you probably walk in the same circles as deeper friends and hence already know most of the same people. Casual friends are more likely to help you make unique connections.

The *fourth level* is a close friend. A close friend is someone you've shared some level of vulnerability with. You've spent time "doing life together." You likely share something personally important with this person—maybe a religious faith or a political affiliation or childhood memories. You really enjoy them and trust them in a way that allows you to put down your guard when you're together. If you were to move to a new city, this friendship would remain a part of your network of connections. Even across different states, you'd likely make time for regular phone calls.

Finally, an intimate friend is your *fifth level* of relationships. This requires really knowing someone, likely over the course of several years, and it probably involves going through some significant life events together. This is the type of relationship in which you feel most fully yourself, trusting that you can share anything without reservation. And, the same is true in reverse: the other person knows that they can share freely with you, without fear of judgement or repercussions. With intimate friends, you not only share the positive achievements of life, but you also share the fears and failures that inevitably arise. This is truly an intimate relationship.

In life, you will have lots of acquaintances with fewer casual friends, even fewer close friends (up to ten), and just a handful of intimate friends—likely three or less. You can't be this close to everyone, nor should you try.

Moving through these levels of relationships requires relating to one another with a high EI. If you don't put in the effort, relationships will never move beyond an acquaintance. Specifically, moving through these levels requires three things: intentionality, mutuality, and awareness.

Becoming more than just an acquaintance or a casual friend with someone requires *intentionality*. It involves purposeful thinking. Start by acknowledging, "I would like to become close friends with this person," then take the time to get to know them, and finally, actively seek ways to share life together. Maybe if you know that jogging is something this person likes to do, and you've been wanting to improve your exercise, then you should suggest running together. Intentionally participating in an activity together will help grow and develop that relationship over time.

Mutuality is also required. If you're interested in growing a relationship beyond just an acquaintance or casual friendship but the other person isn't, it's not going to go anywhere. There has to be a shared interest in getting to know someone in order for that relationship to deepen.

Lastly, deepening relationships involves an *awareness* of the relationship—where you think it's at and where the other person thinks it's at. If you think you're at a Level 4 and the other person thinks you're at a Level 3, then you're at a Level 3. You may feel like the other person is your best friend, but if they're not inviting you that deeply into their life, then you're likely just casual friends.

Likewise, it's only when we're aware of the other person that we are able to grow the relationship further. This requires regularly checking in, asking how they're doing, and making a point to stay in touch. Challenging experiences can bring awareness to our relationships. When my mom passed away in a car accident, there were some people who I was just casual friends with and I didn't reach out to them in the midst of this grief. Those relationships faded away, to the point of becoming strangers. At the same time, others who were already close friends took it upon themselves to reach out even more to me during this time of traumatic loss. One of those friends was Micah.

My brother-in-law had introduced me to him years prior, and we had become acquaintances around video games as teenagers. Later in life, we started hanging out more, becoming casual friends, going through our shared experiences of starting new relationships and breakups, and sharing desires and aspirations in life. Then, when I lost my mom, Micah was one of the close friends who showed up for me. He was there for me when I desperately needed it. I literally cried on his shoulder, and he consoled me.

Later, something traumatic happened in Micah's life, and it was my turn to be there for him. These shared experiences of increasing intimacy and support over the course of more than twenty years assures me that I know I can call on Micah when I need to.

> ## REMEMBER:
>
> ## BEING UNAWARE OF WHERE WE STAND WITH FRIENDS WILL LEAVE A RELATIONSHIP STATIC, FROZEN AT THE LEVEL OF ACQUAINTANCE OR CASUAL FRIEND.

Being unaware of where we stand with friends will leave a relationship static, frozen at the level of acquaintance or casual friend. One of the primary obstacles that prevents people from moving beyond just a casual friendship is the fear of rejection if others see us for who we truly are. This is a well-founded fear— we've all been vulnerable at some point only to be rejected. But we can never gain deep relationships without taking the risk of being hurt.

We will spend more time in the next chapter talking about the work of maintaining friendships. But for now, let's turn to the social skills necessary for building new ones—moving from stranger to acquaintance to casual friend to close friend to, ultimately, intimate friends. These are the social skills you find in anyone with high EI.

SOCIAL SKILLS

Having a high EI requires mastering certain social skills, sometimes called "soft skills." These include everything we do in our interactions with others: from active listening and reading nonverbal cues to speaking clearly and maintaining eye contact. Every interaction we have with other people is regulated by our soft skills. My friend Steve Gutzler, who works in leadership development, says soft skills have hard-edged value. Sometimes they're de-valued in the business world, but they ultimately produce value.

Our social skills, good or bad, are on display whether we think they are or not. The better your social skills, the more likely you'll be able to recognize the strengths and weaknesses of your own social skills. The worse yours are, the more likely you'll be ignorant of what is obvious to others.

Take road rage, for example. We see it in someone's hand gestures, the way they speed up toward someone they're upset with, or by the way they shout at other cars. These are all visible examples of someone who neither knows nor cares about social skills, which demonstrates their low EI. Or take people's behavior on social media. Like road rage, people say things virtually—book reviews, YouTube comments, and social media blasts—that they'd never say face to face. The technology provides a level of anonymity that draws out low EI behavior, resulting in harmful speech and behavior.

A positive example of soft skills is seen when a police officer talks someone down from a bridge. With caution, the police officer approaches and begins to engage the person in conversation. Finally, after some time of listening and encouragement, we can see the other person coming down safely. Unlike road rage and people's behavior on social media, this is an example of someone visibly demonstrating high EI.

As you can see, social skills are not only visible, they have a powerful impact on our lives—in some cases, they are a matter of life and death!

SOFT SKILLS FOR CAREER SUCCESS

In his research on Emotional Intelligence, Dr. Goleman recognized that employees who have mastered soft skills, including discipline, drive, relatability, and empathy are more likely to stand out from the crowd. The reverse is also true—those who fail at soft skills also stand out, but for the wrong reasons.

Research conducted by The Center for Creative Leadership showed that 75 percent of careers were harmed when employees could not adapt to change, cultivate trust, lead teams during difficult periods, or deal with interpersonal issues.

Some employers find ways to consider EI in hiring. They rightly assume that the higher a person's EI, the better a leader or coworker they will be. Measuring EI, however, is tricky, and often goes without standardized testing.

A number of EI measurements have begun to show up in recent years, but many of them have not yet received enough evaluation to be deemed valid. One little-known test that is well regarded is called the Mayer-Salovey-Caruso Emotional Intelligence Test (MSCEIT), named after the EI model founded by Psychologists Dr. Peter Salovey and Dr. John Mayer. This assessment involves answering 141 questions. Unfortunately, the MSCEIT has not caught on, and it remains largely unknown by most people. But this much is clear: employers recognize the importance of EI in the workplace.

Consider for a moment a supervisor who can't read their supervisees. They don't understand their frustration. Or, just as calamitous, they don't understand their joy. The low EI supervisor won't try to help the supervisee overcome their frustration, leading almost inevitably to failure. Or, not recognizing the joy and satisfaction the supervisee feels for the job they have done, the supervisor will fail to give them the proper recognition, almost guaranteeing that the overlooked employee will start looking for work elsewhere.

Any way you look at it, having a high EI and mastering social skills are crucial to workplace advancement. The same is true in one's personal life.

PARENTING AND SOCIAL SKILLS

Think of the impact parenting has on children. When a parent with low EI is caring for their child using poor social skills, it's likely to create harmful habits that can last for years.

As a parent, there are areas of my life that I need to grow in before my son picks up on that behavior and it develops in his own life. Likewise, there are things I am intentionally doing to pass on to him. If I want him to clean up after himself, for example, I need to first model that. The same is also true when it comes to language. I am sure you have all seen this: when parents shout, children shout. And, when parents curse, their children also curse. Children follow their parents' lead.

Right now, I'm teaching my son baseball, but it's been a long time since I last played—grade school, in fact. So, I had to go out and buy a glove. I've been learning how to play baseball all over again, so that I can pass this skill on to my son. Likewise, as a parent, understand that learning social skills not only helps your career but it will help you connect with your kids and teach them social skills. Whether it's intentionally teaching our kids behaviors we want to encourage or unintentionally teaching them bad habits, we are always teaching them something. Children emulate their parents.

Likewise, employees emulate their bosses. When we're caught using negative behavior, our immediate response is, "Well, *he* did it!" And, likewise, if it's positive, we point out: "I saw how Mary handled a stressful situation, and I followed her example." This also happens on a peer-to-peer level, where EI and social skills are learned in everyday experiences and interactions. When we meet people for the first time, we mirror one another, participating in a give-and-take exchange where we're both modeling social skills and learning from each other. People are always watching!

NAILING YOUR FIRST IMPRESSION

One of the most important social skills is the ability to make a good first impression. Fail here and you are facing an uphill (but not impossible) battle. Do you struggle with first impressions? Here are some key techniques:

REMEMBER THEIR NAME. "The sweetest sound in the world is the person's own name," Dale Carnegie once said. And he's right. Often people's favorite word is their own name. We make other people feel important when we remember their name, just as hearing our own name gets our attention and makes us feel important. Our names are central to our identity.

> REMEMBER:
>
> **"THE SWEETEST SOUND IN THE WORLD IS THE PERSON'S OWN NAME."** *—DALE CARNEGIE*

When we recognize people by name, we are doing much more than just remembering them: we're recognizing the family that influenced them in critical ways. For many of us, our name is a thread running through our family history. Maybe your name is a reminder of your parents or your grandparents. Your name can recall someone who played an important role in shaping you into the person you are today. All of this is tapped into when someone hears their name. This is why remembering someone's name can create a deep connection.

That's certainly true in our family. I'm named after my Uncle Michael because my mother loved her brother. And my sister named her youngest son Michael, as well, after me. So when I hear my own name, all of those positive feelings come up for me.

Here are a few ways that you can improve on the social skill of remembering people's names when you meet them. After they have introduced themselves, try to use their name three times in normal conversation. If I were to introduce myself to someone at a workshop I'm leading, it might sound something like this:

"Hi, welcome. My name's Mike."

"Hey Mike, I'm Larry."

"*Larry*, it's great to meet you. What brought you to my workshop?"

"Well, I want to work on some of my management skills. I'm directing a new team at work."

"That's awesome, *Larry*. How long have you been in management?"

"About three years, but I've been a technician for a lot longer. I just kept getting promoted, and now I'm managing a brand-new team."

"Great work, *Larry*! So, what kind of work are you in?"

"I'm a coder."

"Coding, okay. Did you go to school for that? Are you self-trained?"

As you can see, I'm engaging Larry in conversation and using his name in natural ways. And, each time I do that, I'm impressing it in my memory. I don't want it to sound forceful or repetitive—Larry, Larry, Larry—so I don't use it every time I speak, but I return to it throughout the conversation.

Afterward, write down their name and link it with a memorable characteristic or something you learned about them in conversation. Maybe it's that Larry is a coder, or that he worked his way up to management. Then, aim to have a follow-up conversation within a week, be it on email, phone, or in-person—and make sure you remember their name when you do! Do all this, and you're much more likely to create a lasting connection.

EYE CONTACT. Eye contact has long been understood as essential for interpersonal connection. Prolonged eye contact releases phenylethylamine, a chemical associated with feelings of attraction. When you're speaking with others, you aren't necessarily looking for phenylethylamine, but you are looking for connection. Eye contact energizes you and encourages continued communication.

One of the common "first impression mistakes" people make is appearing not to be interested in the other person. This is frequently caused by not making eye contact—whether intentionally or unintentionally. Sometimes we are not even aware of the fact that we have trouble maintaining eye contact in conversation. But once we start focusing on it, we will quickly realize the difference it makes. (*Important note:* This is not true in all cultures. In some, prolonged eye contact can be seen as rude or threatening. Be sure to do your research!)

> ## REMEMBER:
>
> ## AVOIDING EYE CONTACT CAN RUIN THE CHANCES OF A GOOD CONNECTION BEFORE IT GETS OFF THE GROUND.

Where our eyes look tells others what we're paying attention to. And if we're attending to anything other than the person we're meeting, it communicates that something else is more important than them. If we're in a conversation, and we're looking around the room, this will tell the other person that we're uninterested in them. Again, avoiding eye contact, intentionally or unintentionally, can ruin the chances of a good connection before it ever gets off the ground.

I used to go to a church that regularly held conferences. At these conferences, I noticed two people who both worked for the church but who had vastly different connection styles: Sam and Jose. Sam was always interested in looking around to see who was there. Even in conversation, he would look beyond you, making you feel as though you were unimportant. In contrast, Jose had a way of making you feel seen and heard, as though you were the most important person in the room. In conversation, he would always hone in on you, even pulling you off to the side to talk, removing any possible distractions.

What if someone else joins the conversation? Shift your body 45 degrees so that you can welcome the new person in, while maintaining a connection with the first person. This will not only make the new conversation partner feel included, but it also ensures that you don't come across as distracted.

Since the global COVID-19 pandemic began in 2020, virtual communication on Zoom calls and Microsoft Teams meetings has become standard. In fact, at the time of this writing, 11 million virtual meetings are held each day. Unfortunately, we have not adjusted well to this way of communicating. In a wide survey, 69 percent of participants said they feel this has become a tremendous obstacle.

My next book will explore virtual communication in depth. In coaching well over 500 people in 2020, I constantly observed that while most Zoomers now know how to unmute and mute themselves, they still don't know where to look or how to hold themselves. The majority of people I've interacted with are acting like they are still working with a computer, not speaking with another person. Knowing what we've lost, is it any wonder that 69 percent of Zoomers feel disconnected—and, therefore, de-energized?

In our era of Zoom meetings and FaceTime calls, eye contact is still critical to establishing a connection with others. But this gets tricky when it comes to virtual meetings, right? If we're connecting over a computer or phone, then my eyes will naturally go to your face on my screen. But if I'm looking at your face, then it will appear that I'm not making eye contact with you.

Maybe you've noticed this when you were in a virtual meeting and the other person's eyes were on the corner of their screen or constantly flicking back and forth from one corner to the other. Are they looking at you or tracking their stocks? Here's the trick to maintaining virtual eye contact: make sure your eyes are on your camera. Of course, this means you have to first know where your camera is! For most, it will be above your screen, in the center of your computer or phone. But that's not always the case. Make sure you can locate it, and that your eyes are fixed on it anytime you're speaking.

If the other person is speaking, feel free to look at their face on your screen. But whenever you're talking, commit to speaking into your camera to show the person on the other line, "I'm speaking to *you*!"

KEEP IT LIGHT. Another key for making strong first impressions is keeping the conversation positive and light. Research shows that moods are contagious. If I'm in a positive mood when we meet, you're likely to feel better yourself, and you'll look back on our interaction with a positive memory. The opposite is also true! If I'm constantly complaining about politics or the weather during our brief interaction, then you're likely to walk away feeling like a dark cloud has followed you— even if those complaints are valid.

It's not just the content that comes across as light or gloomy in conversation. Just as important are our tone of voice and facial expressions. Even if the conversation is light but we're downcast, our nonverbal communication will be louder than what we're communicating verbally.

Those who form strong bonds with others offer warmth, a positive outlook, and even a laugh. Don't be afraid to work in humor and smiles into your first interaction as a way of keeping things light and positive.

One word of caution: sometimes life is hard, and it can take us by surprise. If you're on a call or meeting with someone who is going through a difficult experience, don't feel like you have to cheer them up or solve their problems. Simply listening and affirming their challenging experience, whatever it may be, might just be what they need from you. In fact, as we will talk about more in the next chapter, simply being present will do more to help them at this point than anything else.

NONVERBAL COMMUNICATION

Successful first impressions also require you to be brutally aware of your own nonverbal communication. We have already spent some time on this, but it's worth revisiting in reference to building relationships and making a strong first impression.

"I knew I didn't like him from the first moment I saw him." You've likely heard someone say that. You may have even said it yourself. Here's the thing: it's not entirely true. Yes, our first impression of someone is made in a microsecond. We all have minute facial tics that we cannot control and, when we see them in someone else, they register in our subconscious brains. This process of subconsciously reading others happens outside of our control. The final interpretation can be negative or positive but usually takes a minute to register. We have time (albeit very little) to correct that impression.

Likewise, the whole "You only have one chance to make a good first impression" is also false. Whether the other person subconsciously likes or dislikes you, you can change their mind the minute you open your mouth. Actually, you don't even have to open your mouth. Nonverbal messages work as well. This goes back to body language. Our eyes, nose, mouth, shoulders, head placement, and forehead can all be intentionally and even unintentionally manipulated in ways that communicate something to others. Now, I don't want you to worry about this and make you paranoid, but I do want to help instruct you.

> ### REMEMBER:
>
> ### NONVERBAL CUES PLAY AN IMPORTANT ROLE IN OUR OVERALL SOCIAL SKILLS AND HOW WE MAKE A STRONG FIRST IMPRESSION.

Let's say you're at a networking event and are standing in a corner of the room, away from others. Your eyes are admiring the carpet, not making eye contact with anyone. Your nose is twitching like you're trying to prevent a sneeze. Your mouth is in a neutral position. And your forehead is creased. Do you think someone is going to come over and introduce themselves? At this point, the only thing you aren't doing to turn people off is to have your back to them and your arms crossed!

Instead, if you stand away from the wall, put your cell phone away, look around, make eye contact, smile, have your arms at your sides, and relax your forehead, people will feel much more inclined to approach you. You'll be sending nonverbal signals that tell others, even though you may be too shy to initiate a conversation yourself, you would welcome one. All of these nonverbal cues are playing an important role in our overall social skills and how we make a strong first impression. They are all worth your time to reflect on.

Now that we've covered some critical social skills to help you connect with others, let's consider the four communication styles you're likely to encounter.

COMMUNICATION STYLES

Generally speaking, there are four different communication styles that you're going to come across when you meet others. As you get to know them more, you'll see more of their specific communication style at play. So, keep these in mind even as we move into our next chapter on maintaining relationships.

One of these styles likely describes you better than the others, but you'll be familiar with all of them.

The first communication style is *aggressive*. Aggressive communicators have no trouble saying what they feel and what they need. When someone from an aggressive communication style is speaking, on the phone or in-person, they're going to come across very authoritatively.

"This is just how it is," they might say. Or, "This is just what you have to do." Both their tone and their words are forceful, and they often run over others in their communication. They are the proverbial bull in a China shop. This communication style represents a small portion of the population. However, this type of communicator will be domineering in a relationship and will take up the majority of the speaking time in an interaction.

Next is the *passive* style of communication. Passive communicators often come across as doormats, struggling to communicate what they feel and what they need. Instead of communicating their objections, they simply do what others ask, without any ability to say no. Even if they are an extrovert and enjoy being around other people, passive communicators will be reluctant to speak up around others.

This hesitancy to say what they feel and what they need means that passive communicators often take on more than they should. To make matters worse, they keep doing it—over and over again—even as they feel exhausted and fed up. This process continues until they finally blow up, harming themselves and others in the process.

You also have *passive-aggressive* communication, which is neither entirely aggressive nor entirely passive. It is somewhere in-between. Passive-aggressive communication often occurs indirectly, in hints, subtle statements, and contradictions. Because of this, passive-aggressive communication can often be confusing, and it can lead to breakdowns in relationships—even before they begin. Often, passive-aggressive communicators aren't even aware of what they're doing because it has become so ingrained in their behavior.

You're likely familiar with passive-aggressive communication, either because it was used in your home growing up or because you've experienced it at work. An example is someone saying, on their way out the door, "This carpet is really getting dirty," when they want you to vacuum it. Or, saying in a business meeting, "It seems like you gave Bob more time to complete this project" when they want you to extend their deadline. In both cases, they're not *really* saying what they mean because they are hoping that you'll read between the lines. Unfortunately, most people fall into this category. They might be slightly more passive, or they might be slightly more aggressive, but they fall somewhere in the middle of these two styles because they do not directly say what they mean.

The last communication style is *assertive*. The assertive communicator says what they mean, and they mean what they say. Being an assertive communicator is not contingent on how you feel, but on what is true. And, they say what they need directly, without doing so aggressively.

REMEMBER:

BEING AN ASSERTIVE COMMUNICATOR IS NOT CONTINGENT ON HOW YOU FEEL, BUT ON WHAT IS TRUE.

If the house needs to be cleaned to host others that evening, an assertive communicator will say, "I need you to have the house clean by four o'clock today." Or, in the same business meeting, they will say, "With all my other projects, I don't think that's a realistic deadline. How would you like me to prioritize my time?" Speaking in a clear, concise, and polite way ensures others can hear and understand what you need from them, without being offensive.

Assertive communication is different from aggressive communication in important ways. Being assertive involves standing up for yourself, being self-confident, direct, and, most importantly, kind. Being assertive is not bullying or manipulating others and doesn't involve ultimatums to get others to do what we want. It involves naming what we need without powering over or controlling others. Speaking assertively means not giving vague responses, it is about being clear and direct. It is saying what you mean and meaning what you say.

Often, when people are assertive and they get push back, they do not revert to passive or aggressive communication. I was in a meeting with about thirty people, and we were discussing some different ideas and the group was about to move forward with one. I spoke up and said, "I hear what you're saying, but I think we should do it *this* way."

I spoke my truth kindly, not aggressively but directly. The group paused, considered my suggestion, then went with the original plan. And that was okay. I was confident in what I communicated and how I did it. But, ultimately, the group decided to go a different direction. And I moved with them, without resorting to frustration or trying to control the situation.

Assertive communicators do not always get their way. When they fail to persuade others, assertive communicators remain calm. They try to learn more for next time, and they refuse to use aggressive behavior to control others.

Having these different communication styles in mind will help you navigate your initial and ongoing interactions with others. Taking the time to notice how others approach you will allow you to respond appropriately to their particular communication style, even if it isn't a healthy one. As you notice their style, also focus on your own. Are there ways you can be assertive even in your first interaction? As you've probably observed, being assertive won't always be well received. Sometimes, others won't like what is being said. However, speaking directly and clearly is the most likely way to create healthy connections from the outset of your relationship.

SELF-AWARENESS

In order to develop our EI and connect with others, we must be self-aware. Being self-aware involves knowing both our strengths and our weaknesses. If we don't know our own strengths, we will not be able to grow and develop them; thus, we will be unable to help others master theirs. And, if we are not familiar with our weaknesses, they will continue to grow into a greater hindrance, and we will be surprised when others call us out.

The only way we will grow our EI is when we realize we have areas in our lives that need improvement. Without making light of a serious topic, it's a bit like the start of sobriety. You can't get sober unless you admit that you are, for the sake of argument, an alcoholic. The same is true for other areas of life. If you don't first admit that you have a problem, then you can't begin to solve it. And let's be clear, weak social skills are a problem!

> ## REMEMBER:
>
> ## IF YOU DON'T FIRST ADMIT THAT YOU HAVE A SOCIAL SKILLS PROBLEM, THEN YOU CAN'T BEGIN TO SOLVE IT.

When it comes to social skills, where are you the strongest? What comes most naturally to you in social environments? Is it sharing about yourself? Or, do you find it easier to listen actively while others speak, staying engaged and exploring more after they have shared? Likewise, what is your current growing edge in this area? Where do you need to improve?

Answering these questions requires spending intentional time reviewing your own aptitudes. This self-reflective work may sound intimidating if you haven't spent much time here. This is hard work, but it will pay off in massive ways if you commit to it!

Now that we have spent some time covering the different stages of relationships, the social skills required for making new friendships, and the various communication styles you'll encounter when you do, I want to encourage you to go for it! Seek out new friendships in your life.

If you have an acquaintance you would like to get to know better, invite them out for coffee. What's the worst that can happen? They can say no. So what? They can also say yes, and you'll be on your way to building what could become a very meaningful friendship in your life. Confidently seek out ways to build new friendships this week.

APPLYING YOUR EI

- What social skills are you most proud of in yourself? Make a point of reminding yourself of these before meeting new people so you can build on them.

- What two specific social skills would you like to improve on in the next month? Write them down and make a point of evaluating them after each interaction. Think of specific ways you can improve them and measure your progress after a month.

- Which communication style best describes you? Are you happy with that answer? How can you become more assertive?

CHAPTER 8:
MAINTAINING

If you're old enough, you remember caravan road trips prior to smartphones and GPS. "Just follow me," was a recipe for disaster. So much could go wrong. If the leader wasn't paying attention or if the follower got pulled over (because the leader was speeding), you might never make it to your destination. Moving from "them" to "us" takes more than one interaction. It requires building and maintaining a relationship and keeping the destination in sight.

While doing work for my Master's program, I was very busy. I was working full time and was taking many classes, so I had to be very intentional about my friendships. On my wall, I posted a typed list of friendships in my life, printed on orange paper. This list included three different categories: my top ten friendships, my top five, and my top three. These were all people I wanted to make sure to touch bases with at least once a month, and I had a plan for doing so. The point is, without intentional effort, people will drift in and out of your life.

One guy I know scrolled to the bottom of his list of text messages every day, and he would text the person he found there. This was his way of making sure to check in with those he hadn't spoken with for a while. Of course, there would be others that he would be texting with every day, but this made sure he was reaching out to those he may have otherwise missed.

REMEMBER:

WITHOUT INTENTIONAL EFFORT, PEOPLE WILL DRIFT IN AND OUT OF YOUR LIFE.

I've been friends with Micah for 25 years, but we now have to be even more intentional about making time for each other since we now live in different states. We are both busy with work, and we are both now fathers to little children. Without this level of intentionality in maintaining our friendship, it would easily drift away to a more distant relationship. Once we have built meaningful relationships, the work doesn't stop. It simply shifts. It still take's intentional effort and work—being present with others when they need us, spending regular time together, and finding ways to help them manage their emotions.

BEING PRESENT

In 2005, my sister went into the hospital to deliver her twin girls. She left her three older children with my mom, who would be looking after them. They were riding in the backseat of my mom's car, driving down the highway in the Kitsap Peninsula in Washington State, when my mom's car accidentally crossed the median and struck a semi-truck in oncoming traffic. She died immediately, on impact. My niece was flown to Harborview Medical Center in Seattle to be treated. After six days, she was released. Her brother was knocked unconscious, leaving a gash on his cheek. My other niece witnessed the entire scene.

My grandmother called to share that my mother had died. I immediately fell to my knees in my office and began crying, devastated by this unimaginably difficult news. When I let my employer know what had happened, eyes still puffy from crying, he encouraged me to take off all the time I needed. I drove to Seattle to check on my niece. As a family, we waited together to see if she would survive and be able to leave the hospital. Thankfully, she recovered fully. As of this writing, she is in medical school.

This was a traumatic time in our family's life. I was single at the time, so often my evenings were spent alone working or studying. During that season of life I had two friends, Collin and Brandon, who regularly reached out. Brandon, a father of three, came over and stayed at my house the first night. Collin stayed over the following three.

When Collin arrived, I offered to make up the couch for him to sleep on, but he insisted on sleeping on my bedroom floor. I remember talking with him in the early morning hours of those first few days, when I would wake up in the middle of the night. Sometimes, he would just listen. Other times, he would put his arm around me. He was especially present with me.

That empathetic support I received from these two friends (and others) was so meaningful to me. It helped me respond to my grief in healthy, helpful ways.

Often, we're prone to trying to solve other people's problems, rather than simply being present with them. When I was overwhelmed with grief, Brandon and Collin offered a profound lesson in the difference simply being present can make.

The ancient Jewish practice of sitting shiva is another example of our need for others to be present when we are struggling. This is a key aspect of maintaining relationships. The Hebrew word, *shiva*, translates into English as "seven." It describes the week-long period in Judaism of mourning at home with relatives after a loved one's burial. This extended time together, without disruption from work or other responsibilities, not only gives space for the experience of grief, it also recognizes our need for others to be present with us as we process and talk about all that we're feeling.

Sitting shiva dates all the way back to ancient Israel. In the biblical book of Job, Job's friends are present with him in his grief, literally sitting with him for days, as he mourns the death of his family and the loss of his livelihood. And they do a great job—that is, until they open their mouths!

When his friends were able to be present with Job in his grief, mirroring his grief by tearing their clothes in response to his lament, they were offering Job the empathetic presence he needed. In Job's case, as in my own, other people's presence can transform our experience from being overwhelmed to finding healing. The takeaway is clear: when friends and family are overwhelmed, you don't always need to say something, but you must always be present.

REMEMBER:

WHEN FRIENDS AND FAMILY ARE OVERWHELMED, YOU DON'T ALWAYS NEED TO SAY SOMETHING, BUT YOU MUST ALWAYS BE PRESENT.

REGULAR TIME

In addition to being present with friends and family when they're going through difficult experiences, maintaining relationships requires spending regular time together. Simply checking in, even when nothing special is going on, is a way of showing others that we care, and that they are important to us. Never has this been more true than in 2020, when pandemic restrictions meant so many were feeling lonely and isolated.

Some of my friends seem to have a special radar that notifies them when I need to be reached out to, always calling or texting at just the right time. Maybe you have friends or family like that. But even when I'm not in particular need of a call, I always feel better when someone I love reaches out simply to check in. I'm sure you feel the same. Knowing what a difference this makes in our own life can be a helpful motivation to make sure we are reaching out to others regularly, even if it's just for a quick phone call. Those "random" calls will encourage others that they are important, valued, and loved. And, who knows? You may just happen to be the one reaching out when they need it most!

Of course, we can't always be checking in on our friends or spending regular time together. Life's busyness will mean we have to say "No" to an offer to get together or catch up with a call. One word of warning here: be careful how many times you say "No" to the same person's requests. Too many times might result in unintentionally sending the wrong message. Our family recently moved into a new area, and we are trying to build friendships during COVID restrictions—no easy feat! There's a guy who lives down the street in our neighborhood who invited us out shortly after we moved in, and we had to say "No." Shortly afterward, he invited us out again, and we had to pass again. After a couple times, he said, "The ball's in your court."

Now, most people don't say that. After two or three times, most people assume you're not interested. In friendships, you have to make sure you're saying "Yes" more than you're saying "No." Otherwise, your response becomes an assumed "No." My wife and I were talking about this during our time in Washington State. We had a group of friends that was trying to include us, but it just wasn't working out for us. After a couple of No's, we responded with our schedule and asked if there was any availability on those dates. That intentional step showed that we were interested in sharing life together, even if their attempts to connect had been unsuccessful.

This practice of prioritizing relationships and intentionally finding ways to spend regular time together is an important aspect of exercising Emotional Intelligence in order to maintain relationships for the long-term.

MANAGING OTHERS' EMOTIONS

Sometimes, the most helpful response to others who are going through a difficult experience is to simply be present. However, there are times when they can use some help. Those who successfully connect with others are not only intentional about checking in, they're able to discern when a helpful response is needed, and they make themselves available.

One of the primary reasons those with a high EI make effective leaders is because they are able to identify and manage other people's emotions. Whether you're a politician, a CEO, a religious leader, or just a good friend, being able to guide others' emotions is a central part of effective human connection. Let me give you an example.

Ben has just arrived ten minutes late to a meeting that you're leading. He is clearly upset about something. His face is agitated, and he is making frustrated remarks under his breath. Ben's late entrance and agitation have disrupted the meeting you're trying to lead. How do you respond?

Managing others' emotions is important not just for managers and business leaders; it is an important part of having a high EI, and it is core to building and maintaining healthy relationships. In fact, Psychologist Daniel Goleman calls handling others' emotions "the fine art of relationships." Effectively responding to and managing others' emotions builds on the work of knowing yourself and managing your own emotions. It also involves being able to recognize and empathize with others' emotions—the work we covered in Part One and Part Two of this book. When you experience someone else's frustration, you must first be able to separate your own emotional response from theirs. Then, while maintaining control of your own emotions, you must identify and empathize with their emotional experience.

Let's return to the example of Ben's disruptive entrance. The first step in effectively managing Ben's emotions involves making sure that his agitation and disruption does not control your own emotional response.

REMEMBER:

EMOTIONS ARE CONTAGIOUS—
A LEADER'S FIRST JOB IS TO MAINTAIN
THEIR OWN COMPOSURE.

As you know, emotions are contagious. People can bring either positive or negative emotions into any setting, which has the potential to change how everyone else will react. Without thinking about it, someone treating you with gratitude is more likely to make you grateful toward others. Likewise, someone treating you with a short temper can tempt you to respond with impatience yourself. For better or worse, other peoples' emotions shape our emotions—unless we're intentional about controlling them. As a high EI leader and relator, your first job is to maintain your own composure. Ben's agitation must not become contagious for you. While remaining centered, you can now address Ben directly.

"Thanks for joining us, Ben," you can say. "I can see something is bothering you. I'm sorry about that. Is that something you would like to talk about after this meeting?"

Acknowledging Ben's presence and how he feels can help diffuse the tension that has just entered the room, which has now disrupted everyone's attention. This also encourages Ben that someone sees that he is not doing well and is willing to help. Assuming Ben appreciates the offer, he should now be better able to focus. And you'll now be able to redirect everyone else's attention to the topic at hand.

Those with a high EI, who can identify and influence others' emotions, are not only effective leaders, they are more popular and sought out as a valued member of their team, family, or organization. In addition, those with a high EI are more likely to be introduced to new work opportunities, as they effectively maintain healthy relationships with others. They are also able to maintain relationships when potential challenges arise, using their high EI to address difficult issues—a topic we'll spend more time on in the next chapter.

APPLYING YOUR EI

- Who are the three people who have been most present to you during crises in your life? What did they do that was especially helpful for you? What do you want to learn from them, and offer to others?

- What relationships in your life could benefit from more regular interactions? List three to five people—friends, family, or otherwise—who you would like to do a better job of staying in touch with and commit to doing so once or twice a month.

- Who is someone in your life who has helped you manage your emotions? Is it a counselor or a friend, perhaps? What have they done that has been helpful? What can you learn from them as you offer others help with their own emotions?

CHAPTER 9:
SOLVING

Back to the road trip analogy. Thanks to everyone being responsible with their own cars, skillfully navigating the crowded freeway, and maintaining good communication with everyone else in the party, you all arrive safe and sound at the campground and start setting up the tents. But then the rain starts coming down. The person assigned to make the first dinner left their ice chest at home. The campground has run out of firewood. As you sit around an empty fire pit eating power bars for dinner, tempers begin to flare. You realized that what happens over the next couple days will either pull the group apart or else bring you all together.

———————————

When I was 19 years old, I was dating a girl named Kristy. We dated for about three months, and I was really into her. But, as often happens, we broke up, and I was having a hard time with it. In fact, I was holding out hope that we would end up back together.

A few months later my friend Micah came in with a swagger, his cool car, and a well-paying job. He began dating Kristy. The wound from our breakup was still fresh at this point. Now, I was even more hurt.

Micah could tell I was upset. I wasn't really talking to him. And, when I was, I was acting in a passive-aggressive way.

"I can't believe you would do that!" I finally said, after letting things boil up inside of me for a while. "You *knew* I was still interested in her!"

Thankfully, Micah's EI kicked in. He realized the aftermath of his decision—he was going to jeopardize a friendship that he valued—and was direct with me.

"Mike, I am into Kristy," he told me. "But we just started dating, and I value our friendship more."

In this conversation, Micah modeled everything we have talked about so far. He brought a high level of self-awareness, both in terms of his actions and his values. He also brought empathy, allowing himself to feel what I was feeling. In short, he demonstrated a high EI in this conversation that had a significant potential for conflict. But, because of how he approached it, we were able to have a great conversation. After listening to me and sharing how he felt, Micah made the decision to stop seeing her before their relationship grew any more. That meant a lot to me.

As a result of his decision, our friendship grew, and 25 years later he is one of my best friends. In fact, he and his wife—*not* Kristy!—are close friends with me and my wife (also not Kristy!) And our children are now friends, as well. But I trace our closeness today back to this time where he used EI to relate to me and to work through this potentially explosive situation. Specifically, he used EI to solve an issue *before* it got in the way of our relationship. EI helps solve a minor problem before it becomes a major problem.

REMEMBER:

EI HELPS SOLVE A MINOR PROBLEM BEFORE IT BECOMES A MAJOR PROBLEM.

Think about a plumbing issue in your home. It may begin with a tiny leak under your kitchen sink, but if it's not addressed, it will become bigger and bigger until it erupts, destroying dry wall and flooring, and creating far more trouble than if you would have addressed it sooner. What was initially a small issue can, and will, become a major one if not carefully responded to.

The same is true of our relationships. Sooner or later, every relationship comes to a point where challenges must be addressed. Whether it's a friendship, a colleague, a family member, or otherwise, we all face issues with others that require a high EI to navigate well. EI can help solve a little problem before it becomes a big problem.

In this chapter, we will conclude with a series of social skills you need to navigate any number of issues you may face when connecting with others. We will talk about how to receive and reframe criticism. We will cover ways to successfully deliver hard feedback to ensure positive improvement. And I will give you the tools you need to effectively address and resolve conflict when it arises, helping ensure you're able to navigate to a healthy solution.

It may help keep a specific relationship challenge in mind while you're reading this chapter. This will ensure that this chapter doesn't remain an abstract realm but becomes practical. Let's start with the experience of receiving negative feedback.

REFRAMING CRITICISM

One of the primary ways we get into conflict with others involves receiving criticism. And this isn't just reserved for the workplace. Even at home, we often struggle to take criticism well. I know that this has been my own challenge.

Part of handling criticism is understanding ourselves, which we covered in Part One. When we know our own strengths and weaknesses, we are less likely to be surprised or offended when others bring up areas that we need to work on. Before we can respond to criticism from others in healthy ways, we must be able to identify areas for growth in our own life. Of course, it helps if we're already actively working on them.

REMEMBER:

THINK OF CRITICISM AS AN OPPORTUNITY
TO GROW.

Once you're growing in self-awareness of both your strengths and your weaknesses, the next step is learning how to reframe how you receive criticism. Instead of thinking of criticism as a time to put up your defenses, think of it as an opportunity to grow. Rather than assume that someone is criticizing to attack you, reframe their comments as an opportunity to improve.

The beloved late comedian Jerry Lewis was once asked what he thought of critics. He basically said that there are two types. The first is the critic who knows nothing about the art, knows nothing about the industry, cares nothing about the art, and cares nothing about the industry. Those critics, he said, fall under the old adage, "Those who can, do. Those who can't, teach. And those who can't do either become critics." He got the laugh, and he made his point.

Lewis went on to talk about the second type of critic—the person who knows the art, knows the industry, and genuinely cares. Even if you disagree with their critique, you ignore their feedback at your own peril.

REMEMBER:

"THOSE WHO CAN, DO. THOSE WHO CAN'T, TEACH. AND THOSE WHO CAN'T DO EITHER BECOME CRITICS." –JERRY LEWIS

When it comes to receiving criticism, start by giving yourself time to ask some questions. *Does this person know what they're talking about—the industry, the specific project, or otherwise?* Second, ask yourself, *Does this person care—again, about the industry, the work, or, and equally important, about me?* If the answer to these questions is yes, then pay attention to what they are sharing. Being able to receive and respond well to criticism as an opportunity for growth is key to helping you improve.

I was working with one client for some time when she had a major public speaking project coming up. Public speaking is my background and expertise, and my client was doing one thing that I knew we would need to address. I also knew it was going to make for a difficult conversation.

So, I paused, and I told her that she would need to work on improving in this particular area. Now, this feedback was tough for her to receive. But, I cared for her, I clearly knew the industry, and that came through. Because of this, she was able to hear from me in a way that allowed her to overcome this public speaking issue and improve her delivery.

Now, if the answer to the questions that Jerry Lewis posed is no, then control your emotions and respond with gratitude all the same. If they don't know what they're talking about, and if they don't actually care, then it might not be in your best interest to follow their advice—but you don't have to take their criticism to heart in order to respond well. You can always control your actions and your words, no matter the audience.

EMOTIONAL TRIGGERS

Some critics are worth listening to and some aren't. But no matter who it's coming from, criticism is hard to hear—especially if it's valid. That is why, in addition to being self-aware and reframing criticism, you have to pay attention to your emotional triggers. You must be able to identify them beforehand and manage them when they arise.

Anything can set someone off. For example, tone of voice can do it for some of us. Maybe you had a parent or adult in your life who always used a particular tone of voice when you did something wrong. If you hear a similar tone in others when they're offering feedback, that can immediately bring you back to your childhood—making you shut down, feel like a failure, or, worse, blow up. Noticing in advance that a particular tone of voice can remind you of your childhood can help you understand and control your emotional response.

Similarly, some of us have a special place in our heart for gossip—and not in a good way! If we have been hurt by gossip, or know of someone else who has, we will have little patience for it. If you receive negative feedback in a roundabout way, rather than directly, that, too, can cause your emotions to flare up.

Without giving gossip a pass, simply noticing that this behavior causes such internal frustration in you can help you be prepared when it arises: to identify your emotions, to calm yourself down and regain control, to identify the source of your emotions, and then to address the feedback *directly*.

Body language can also be a trigger for some of us. Someone folding their arms over their chest during a meeting can build a barrier, putting a halt on what you're trying to share. Or, if they don't maintain eye contact and look at other people while you're talking to them, this can not only be a distraction, it can set you off. (I know it does for me!) Knowing that these particular actions can be a trigger can help you respond more calmly when they happen.

All of these are common emotional triggers. Maybe you see yours here, maybe yours is something else. Knowing your emotional triggers in advance is key to maintaining control over them and responding well when they happen.

BODY LANGUAGE

Let's spend some more time on that last emotional trigger: body language.

When it comes to noticing other people's body language, we must realize how easily it can be misinterpreted—even when we're paying attention! For example, someone may be crossing their arms in a meeting. It's not to build a barrier between you, but their back hurts and crossing their arms helps alleviate their discomfort. Or, they may be looking away while you're speaking not because they don't want to listen to you, but because something important is happening elsewhere. They may have noticed a conflict that is about to explode and you hadn't even noticed because you were focused on their distracted look.

Instead of taking personal offense, a person with high EI will pause and address it directly. "Is something wrong? It seems like it might be," they might ask. Or, better still, "Is everything all right?" By addressing body language directly, we can make sure we're not misinterpreting someone's behavior, which then helps avoid unnecessary conflicts.

REMEMBER:

BY ADDRESSING BODY LANGUAGE DIRECTLY, WE CAN MAKE SURE WE'RE NOT MISINTERPRETING SOMEONE'S BEHAVIOR.

DELIVERING HARD FEEDBACK

Just as receiving criticism is hard, so, too, is delivering it. Pointing out something that an employee needs to improve on can be so uncomfortable for some leaders that they avoid it and make the situation worse. Being able to offer critical feedback in a helpful way is a key mark of effective leaders. Here are several ways you can deliver negative feedback to create positive change.

BUILD CONFIDENCE. The first thing you should do is actively instill confidence in the other person. And part of instilling confidence is stating, very clearly, your intentions at the outset of your meeting.

"Hey, Jefferson. Thanks for taking the time to meet with me today," you might say to introduce the conversation. "I want to talk with you about something I have noticed in our meetings, something I know you can improve."

Stating your positive intentions at the outset—wanting to help them improve—can help alleviate tensions that are in place at the start of the conversation. And, even as you point out where they need to improve, go the extra mile of assuring them that you know they have it in them. A leader with high EI will remind others of what they have already done well, and that they can excel again, rather than dwell on where they have come up short.

The opposite of this approach is the leader who reminds others of their failures in a way that makes it more likely they'll fail again. The teacher who says with a voice of exhaustion, "You're just not getting it," is more likely to find her student struggling with the same mistake on the next assignment, rather than seeing the improvement they're both after.

This is called a self-fulfilling prophecy: when we treat others in a way that actually shapes their behavior in the direction we expect. And self-fulfilling prophecies can work either negatively or positively. Effective leaders recognize the way they can shape others, and they frame their critical feedback in hopeful terms. Comments like "You've got this," or, "You can do it," are doing more than just making others feel good. They're actually creating the very response we want to see.

REGULAR COMPLIMENTS. You've likely heard of the compliment sandwich, which involves "sandwiching" hard feedback between two compliments. This only works if you're regularly complimenting people, otherwise the compliments will feel contrived, so get better at giving compliments before you have to give hard feedback! A good rule of thumb is that people need to hear seven compliments for every one piece of critical feedback.

REMEMBER:

PEOPLE NEED TO HEAR SEVEN COMPLIMENTS FOR EVERY ONE PIECE OF CRITICAL FEEDBACK.

In my own professional journey, I once had a boss who continually gave me almost exclusively negative feedback. He even went so far as saying that major accomplishments of mine were actually failures. This devastated my morale. Later on, that same boss made a switch. He began giving me a lot of positive feedback. That's good, right? Well, yes, but the damage had already been done. I was skeptical because I had heard so much negative feedback from him for so long, I no longer trusted him and didn't want to work for him. Remembering this is essential for any leader: you can't just flip-flop from negative to positive all the time.

You also have to be strategic about *when* to deliver hard feedback. The general rule is: praise in public, correct in private. Overall, become a person who is regularly positive. Reward what you want repeated. Giving compliments regularly makes your employees not only feel *secure*, but it will also make them want to stay and contribute to your mission.

REMEMBER:

REWARD WHAT YOU WANT REPEATED.

BUT VS. AND. When it comes to delivering hard feedback, one of the common approaches is to lead with positive feedback and then switch to the ways they're falling short, using the word "but."

"You're delivering really well over here," a supervisor might say, "*but…*" And then they move on to delivering something critical. I've been guilty of doing this and have also been on the receiving end of this approach.

I used to have a supervisor who would routinely say, "Here's what you did well, *but…*" Every time he did that, what came after the word "but" was all I heard after he had finished talking. This happened so often that whenever I heard him use the word "but," I knew what was going to come next, and that I wouldn't like it! The word "but" became associated in my mind with negative feedback. Without realizing it, he was training me to ignore everything he said before the "but." This is why psychologists, politicians, and business leaders alike encourage you to get rid of the word "but." It blocks out an essential part of the message you were trying to deliver—the positive feedback—rather than delivering both the positive feedback *and* identifying the negative behavior that needs to be addressed. Likewise, the word "but" can cause someone to stop listening to what's coming *next*. This is especially true if they have been trained to associate the word "but" with negative feedback or bad news.

Make sure that when you're delivering hard feedback, you're moving from positive examples to critical feedback using the word "and." Unlike the word "but," which dismisses what's just been said, the word "and" acknowledges what has just been said, and it adds to or expands the message you're delivering.

This simple tweak in your communication will tell the other person that both their good work *and* the issue that needs to be addressed are true—not simply one or the other. It will completely change the conversation.

SPECIFIC & PERSONAL. Another way you can maintain high EI and use positive social skills when it comes to delivering hard feedback is to be specific and personal. Rather than generalize your critique, or—even worse—universalize their mistake, focus on the specific way they failed to meet expectations and explain clearly how it needs to be improved.

If you're addressing an issue of an employee delivering late work, for example, make sure you name the specific projects that were not completed on time, remind them of when it was needed, and be clear that you will need future projects delivered on time. Being as specific as possible removes any confusion, increases the likelihood of improvement, and helps avoid unnecessary conflict.

You've often experienced the same issue at home. High EI, healthy couples are more likely to avoid making generalizing and universalizing statements when it comes to addressing problems. If the dishes need to be washed and it's the husband's responsibility, a wife with high EI will be specific about the fact that this work needs to be done *now*, rather than pointing out that the husband is "always" leaving messes for others to clean up, or that he "always" leaves the dishes piling up in the sink (even if that's true!). Avoiding generalizing statements when delivering critical feedback and not universalizing negative behavior is key to encouraging the results we want to see in others, whether it's at work or at home.

REMEMBER:

BEING AS SPECIFIC AS POSSIBLE WHEN DELIVERING HARD FEEDBACK INCREASES THE LIKELIHOOD OF IMPROVEMENT.

When you're being specific and personal in delivering hard feedback, it's best to have two specific examples. One instance might be an anomaly or nitpicking, but two are worth addressing.

I had an employee that I noticed was late. This isn't that unusual. We all experience situations that cause us to be late from time to time. So, it wasn't until I noticed him arriving late on two occasions that I addressed his tardiness.

CRITICAL QUESTIONS. Before you move ahead toward a solution, ask the other person a couple of questions. First, after offering two specific examples of the issue you're addressing, ask if they're aware of this issue. Someone who has a habit of interrupting colleagues in meetings, for example, may not even realize what they are doing. Remember: EI begins with awareness. Help them become emotionally intelligent by making sure they are aware of the issue, even if you need to help them become aware of it, before moving forward with the conversation.

Then, once they're clear on the issue and when it happened, ask why they think this specific issue might be happening. Again, if we're dealing with someone who is routinely interrupting their colleagues, give the other person an opportunity to explain *why* they think it is happening. Maybe their reason is that this is simply how they were raised, with family members constantly speaking over one another. Or, maybe they are feeling unheard, and they are working hard to speak up, even at the cost of speaking over others. Whatever their reason, giving them an opportunity to explain themselves, before working together on a solution, will help ensure you're addressing the root issue, not just the surface level concern.

To go one step further, after you have listened to the other person explain why they think this negative behavior is happening, and you have reflected that reason back to ensure you heard correctly, give the other person an opportunity to dig deeper.

"So, it sounds like this is how you're used to communicating," you might say.

"Yeah, that's just how I was raised," he responds.

"Okay, I get that. We all have our expectations about how we should interact. What else do you think might be causing this?"

Often the first answer that comes to mind isn't the only possible one. Sometimes, it's not even the best one. Giving people more time to think about alternative explanations can help get at something that is even more significant. And, by asking an open-ended question like, "What else?", you avoid giving the other person an easy out by encouraging them to think about what is really going on.

> ## REMEMBER:
>
> ## GIVING PEOPLE MORE TIME TO THINK ABOUT ALTERNATIVE EXPLANATIONS CAN HELP GET AT SOMETHING THAT IS EVEN MORE SIGNIFICANT.

When you've given this space for reflection, you both might be surprised at what comes up. Maybe the real issue isn't just that they were raised in a household where people constantly spoke over one another. Maybe the real issue is impatience, which they need to work on so they can hear from others. By giving this extra opportunity, you'll have helped this person identify the real root cause of an issue.

COLLABORATIVE SOLUTIONS. After you have given them an opportunity to think more about the real cause, offer to help them come up with a practical solution. This is another mark of a high EI leader. Instead of just delivering negative feedback and leaving it up to the other person—or dictating what they should do—effective leaders come alongside others and offer creative and actionable solutions.

If you have perspective on what went wrong, you likely have a helpful perspective on how to improve things. Maybe it's sharing an example of something that has created positive change for you in the same area. If your intern's issue is time management, for example, then sharing a software or app that you have personally found helpful may be just the help they need. Helpful suggestions will not only show that you believe they can improve, it will offer them the practical next steps they need to get there.

BE PRESENT. Next, a high EI leader delivers tough feedback in a personal and present way. Since delivering critical feedback can be uncomfortable, many leaders will share it in an impersonal and distant way. Sending a frustrated email after work hours or at the end of the week, when you're unlikely to interact with that person, is a sure sign that you're more interested in your own comfort than in seeing them improve. And high EI leaders always want to see others improve!

REMEMBER:

HIGH EI LEADERS ALWAYS WANT TO SEE OTHERS IMPROVE!

A leader with high EI will make a point of delivering hard feedback in-person whenever possible. This is a sign of maturity. Of course, meeting in person isn't always possible. Barring an in-person meeting, a leader with high EI will set aside time for a video call.

Maintaining eye contact and showing with your nonverbal cues—including your facial expression and your physical posture—that you care for the other person, even while you're naming areas for improvement, will increase the likelihood that your feedback is taken to heart. Meeting in-person or on a video call, rather than sending an email at the end of the week or after hours, will also give the other person room to ask for clarification. This will also help ensure that your feedback is fully understood, making it more likely to be acted on.

A POSITIVE EXAMPLE:
DELIVERING HARD FEEDBACK TO MATTHEW

All of these steps can be seen in what I did with Matthew when we needed to have a hard conversation. A lot of the success of this story is due to his own ability to listen and take in feedback.

In our working relationship, I praised Matthew regularly and recognized his success over and over again. He was a great employee, and I wanted to make sure he was aware that I noticed the hard work he was putting in to succeed. Since then, he has gone on to remarkable success in his career. In fact, he now owns his own company, where he is thriving.

Yet, there was one time where we were working on a project and Matthew fell short of the timeline. I brought him in to talk about this issue. The first thing I did was to check in.

"Are you doing well?" I asked. "How are things going with you?"

I didn't want to give Matthew negative feedback if he was already going through something difficult in his personal life. There have been times where I've checked in with employees, and they shared that their family was going through a hard time. That's not the time to give negative feedback! That's an important time to listen, to encourage, and to build them up. Taking the time to check in helps avoid the error of delivering hard feedback at the wrong time. (Unless, of course, you're dealing with someone who *always* seems to have something hard going on.)

Back to my conversation with Matthew—after checking in and hearing that things were going well in his life, I gave him some positive feedback in areas where I saw his work excelling.

"Remember when you did that?" I asked him. "You knocked that out of the park! You were fantastic at recruiting and developing other people. Great job!"

And then I got into the hard feedback, beginning with a question to learn more.

"Do you remember the timeline I gave you on this project?" I asked Matthew. This helps to make sure that we're both in agreement before addressing what needs to be corrected.

"Yeah, I remember the timeline," he said.

"Did you meet it?" I asked.

"No, no I didn't."

So, at this point in time, he has already been given his feedback. But I gave him an opportunity to explain more.

"Okay, so can you tell me more about what's going on?" I asked.

As he explained, I actively listened, echoing back to him what he was sharing, making sure that he knew I was hearing him and understood his perspective, before sharing my own.

"Well, here's what I noticed," I told him. "You prioritized *this* aspect, rather than *that* aspect. And, if you remember, I did tell you what you needed to prioritize. Because you didn't do so, you were unable to meet the deadline."

As I explained what I saw happening, Matthew nodded. His response was not anger or frustration, but agreement. So, I continued, moving into what I saw as a solution.

"Here's what I need you to do," I said. Very clearly, I spelled out the next steps that he needed to take. Then I concluded with more positive feedback, reminding Matthew of ways that he has delivered past projects successfully. This was my way of encouraging him. I believed he could still deliver on this project, and I wanted to help him believe in himself.

Matthew left our conversation knowing that I was for him because he regularly received my positive support. He also left this conversation having just heard two positive pieces of feedback, reaffirming his regular experience of my positive support. He also heard something that he needed to correct and had a clear sense of how he could improve. Later on, he came back to me and apologized for missing the deadline and assured me that he would make it right.

So much of Matthew's response comes down to the fantastic person he is. And, even when you're working with fantastic people, there needs to be an intentional effort to make sure the working relationship remains positive.

When you deliver hard feedback, give the critique, lead with concern (for them) and curiosity (for the issue at hand), and give clear feedback on how they can correct the issue. In addition, make sure to end the conversation with positive affirmation. All of this will help others create positive change. It will also help them grow in the process. Remember: high EI leaders always want to help others improve.

REMEMBER:

LEAD WITH CONCERN FOR THEM AND CURIOSITY.

Even if you take all of these steps, of course, there is no guarantee that your feedback will be well received. Conflict may still occur. How can you best address that conflict when it happens?

RESOLVING CONFLICTS

Some conflicts can be resolved before they even begin with a combination of EI, social skills, and proactive attention. Some conflicts, however, are simply unavoidable. But just because a conflict happens doesn't mean it needs to be destructive. Those developing a high EI have helpful, healthy ways to deal with conflict.

Psychologist Susan Heitler offers a helpful three-step approach to resolution: find the source of the problem and discuss potential ideas to address it, explore the source of the conflict, and then determine a mutual solution.[9]

To start, Dr. Heitler encourages taking the time to identify the source of the conflict and to discuss potential ideas to resolve it. Conflicts arise, in large part, because two or more people are looking at the same situation in different ways.

When I was 19, I was working at a popular restaurant bussing tables. One day, my manager called me into his office. One of the waitresses had complained to him that I wasn't cleaning her area as well as others. I was affronted by this—I was working very hard to make sure I was doing my job well and was upset that she would say otherwise. I went straight to her and asked her to come to me next time she had a problem with my work. In response, she went right back to our boss and complained about me again! My co-worker and I clearly had two different perspectives.

---

[9] https://www.psychologytoday.com/us/blog/resolution-not-conflict/201211/what-makes-conflict-how-are-conflicts-resolved

Taking the time to clarify the problem and discuss potential ways to address it is the first step in recognizing that your view isn't the only perspective. It will also open your mind to hearing a better approach. In this particular example, my colleague and I could have very different ideas for a solution, given our different perspectives. Maybe her solution is that I let her know when I have finished busing her table so she can inspect it. My solution, however, might be that she needs to trust that I'm looking out for her tables just as much as everyone else's and that she should come to *me* if there's a problem. Two perspectives and two solutions.

Instead of jumping directly into choosing the best solution, the next step of this conflict resolution process involves taking the time to explore the underlying concern. When we're talking about concerns here, we're talking about the factors that led to the conflict in the first place. Maybe it's an emotion (like frustration or fear), an unmet desire (like recognition), a difficult event (death of a loved one), or something else. If we don't take the time to address the underlying concerns, any solution is bound to fail.

REMEMBER:

IF WE DON'T TAKE THE TIME TO ADDRESS THE UNDERLYING CONCERNS, ANY SOLUTION IS BOUND TO FAIL.

Perhaps my co-worker's underlying concern is that she feels overlooked and not just at work. And if she thinks I'm overlooking her tables, it could be just another area where she feels ignored. It wouldn't be until we take the time to get to the source of her frustration with me that we could discover this. When conflict arises, take the time to dig in and learn more. Rather than react defensively, lead with curiosity. Listen actively, without judgement. And continue to ask questions and reflect what you're hearing until you get to the underlying concern.

"Are you feeling overlooked?" I might ask, after listening to my colleague's concerns. If it turns out that she is, then that's going to influence my suggested solution. I'm going to recognize that I need to make sure she feels seen and noticed, which goes beyond letting her know when her tables are ready. At the same time, our conflict also involves other concerns—namely, mine! Perhaps I felt belittled or patronized by her going directly to my boss. Or, maybe I felt like she was calling me lazy. Both parties' concerns need to be fully considered before moving to the third and final step.

REMEMBER:

WHEN CONFLICT ARISES, LEAD WITH CURIOSITY.

The next step in conflict resolution, according to Dr. Heitler, is to determine a mutually agreeable solution. The word "mutual" is key here. Both parties involved must feel like they have been seen and heard for the solution to work. Begin by summarizing all the concerns involved. Leave nothing out. And, when you think you're done, make sure both parties feel their concerns are fairly represented. Do not move forward until everyone feels seen and understood. Then, remind yourselves of the solutions initially proposed in the first step and ask how those proposed solutions need to be adjusted after hearing everyone's real concerns.

REMEMBER:

BOTH PARTIES MUST FEEL LIKE THEY HAVE BEEN SEEN AND HEARD FOR THE SOLUTION TO WORK.

For example, after hearing that my co-worker is struggling with feeling overlooked, I may tweak my solution and agree to touch bases with her after I finish cleaning her tables. And if I care about her as a person, I would internally commit to acknowledging her good work and giving her kudos in front of others. Similarly, maybe she could empathize with feeling belittled and agree to come to me first. When both parties are tweaking their solutions to reflect the other's concerns, they are acting with high EI and moving toward healthy conflict resolution.

Keeping this helpful three-step approach in your back pocket will save you the stress of trying to figure out how to respond to unavoidable conflicts. The key is maintaining healthy, high EI communication skills, using your positive social skills, and not allowing emotional flare ups or defensive posturing to disrupt this process from moving toward a successful outcome—for *everyone*.

THE DISAGREEABLE CHARACTER: IT'S NOT ABOUT YOU

A conflict resolution plan will help address conflicts when they arise with family, friends, or in the workplace. But that plan may need to be adjusted when you're working with an especially disagreeable character.

Let's imagine there's an employee that everyone agrees is difficult to work with. You know the ones. Always right and everyone else is always wrong. Only one tone of voice: loud. Only one mannerism: aggressive. Their EI is exceptionally low, and they cannot be reasoned with. They are impossible. They live by the rule, "The squeaky wheel gets the oil." So, you either give in and surrender to their demands, or you throw them out.

Since you have high EI and they don't, you realize that there will be consequences either way. It may be easier to give in, but you know that that will embolden them and they'll demand more. But if you throw them out—after all, many companies fire bad employees or (kick out) customers because they aren't worth the aggravation—you know that they'll give you a one-star review on every social media platform known to man. But then your EI kicks in. You realize that they don't just act that way with *you*. They act that way with *everyone*. That means that they have no credibility.

This was the case with Shannon's dad. In 2003, I was running a leadership program for teenagers. Parents would drop off their kids for our two-hour weekly program and then return later that evening to pick them up. One evening, Shannon's dad came in fuming and pacing through the lobby. He was looking for me.

"We need to talk," he said when he found me, interrupting my conversation with several students, his face boiling with frustration. "You need to teach these teenagers about respect! My daughter has no respect, and you need to teach her!"

He was demanding that I teach these students about respect, yet he was acting without any semblance of it himself. He didn't ask if I had time to talk. His tone was deeply disrespectful towards me. He was disrespecting his daughter in front of her peers, and he was disrespecting the students I was meeting with.

Reflecting on the encounter that evening, I thought about his history. He didn't respect police authority, he didn't respect church authority, and he constantly criticized the government. His emotional outburst was born out of his low EI and disrespect for everyone. And yet, shockingly, he was surprised when his own daughter reacted disrespectfully toward him.

So what do you do with a person like this? A leader with high EI will recognize this complete lack of respect isn't reserved for them; it's part of a wider trend. Once you recognize that, it will be much easier, when such an outburst happens, to tell yourself, "Don't take it personally. This isn't about me." When you do that, you'll be able to remain calm, even when you're at the pointy end of their inappropriate behavior. As one leader I know likes to say (internally) when dealing with a person like that, "I'm sorry you're that dysfunctional." He genuinely means it, but doesn't allow that person to affect him.

THE COMPANY GOSSIP

Another character who lacks EI, and is a cancer in any organization, is the company gossip. They make up stories. They exaggerate the truth. They blow things entirely out of proportion. They start and spread rumors that have the potential to destroy lives and careers. But to do that, they have to have an audience.

There are three people involved with any piece of gossip: the gossiper, the audience, and the victim. The audience is also called the facilitator. If there's no audience, there's no gossip—*period*. If a tree falls in a forest and no one is there to hear it, does it make any noise? Of course. But if a gossiper gossips and no one listens…Well, you get the idea.

It can be helpful to understand that the gossiper does not have high EI. They don't know how to interact with people and often resort to gossip because they don't know how else to engage in conversation. Colleagues who have high EI know how to interact, which involves knowing when *not* to listen, and certainly when not to engage. They also know when to tell the gossiper to stop. They know when to walk away, showing their disgust with this behavior and shutting it down in the process. Most importantly, they know one other thing: Today, it's Joe. Tomorrow, it's Jane. And the day after that? It will be them!

The gossiper usually fails to recognize their emotions and realize that they are the problem, choosing instead to blame and focus on others. When their audience tells them, "No thanks" and removes themselves from the conversation, they help the gossiper see the error of their ways and, possibly, guide them toward developing higher EI.

> # REMEMBER:
>
> ## CHOOSE TO BE PART OF THE SOLUTION, NOT THE PROBLEM.

Problem behavior is only corrected when people challenge it. As someone with high EI, choose to be part of the solution, not the problem. Having a high EI involves attending to all the emotional information available and then reasoning your way to a healthy response. EI allows us to dismiss, reject, or ignore unproductive emotions—in others and also ourselves. Those with a high EI are able to avoid interactions that are only going to cause more trouble in the end, while engaging in difficult, yet productive interactions.

HIGH EI & SOCIAL SKILLS BOOSTS OUR REPUTATION

As I pointed out at the start of this chapter, high EI has the power to make a positive impact even in negative situations. If you consider the example of the company gossip or the disagreeable employee, developing your EI and your social skills improves your reputation, and it helps those around you by modeling an alternative solution.

When we walk away from a situation where someone is gossiping about another colleague, we are not only refusing to participate in destroying someone else's reputation, but we are showing our high EI and boosting our reputation in the process. The gossiper, in comparison, is now only harming their own reputation. Those who are working on their EI skills will notice this difference and take note.

The same is true with the disagreeable staff member. When we avoid responding in kind to their angry outburst, our reputation is maintained, and theirs is harmed. Our colleagues with EI will appreciate how we handle the situation. They will learn to develop their EI and their own social skills by watching us. We will help to defuse the situation, and they will learn how to do the same by our example.

When we act with high EI and put our social skills to use, we are not only contributing to our own success, both personally and professionally, but we are also contributing to the success of others'. Others will notice, and they will thank you!

———————————

In the words of *The Princess Bride*, "Life is pain. Anyone who says differently is selling something." It rains on camping trips, we have to deal with difficult employees, you are criticized, moments of conflict arise, and difficult feedback must be given. But a high EI has the power to make these painful situations productive. Why waste the pain?

APPLYING YOUR EI

- One of the biggest sources of conflict is delivering and receiving criticism but conflict can be avoided by reframing it as an opportunity for growth. Think back to a specific time when you received hard feedback: what was one obstacle that stood in the way of you receiving it well? How might you take that same criticism and reframe it into an opportunity for growth? Try to respond that way next time. When you do so, you'll not only improve in this area, but you'll also improve your overall EI.

- Just as receiving negative feedback is challenging, so is delivering it. Which of the tools in this chapter did you find most useful for delivering hard feedback? Commit to including this new tool in your approach the next time and observe the recipient's response. Did it help? If so, how? Seeing improvements can help us become more confident the next time.

- We are not always able to avoid conflict. Which aspect of conflict resolution is most difficult for you? Rather than waiting for the next conflict, focus on a past one. How might things have turned out differently if you had used the tools in this chapter? Simply imagining using a different approach in past experiences will help you respond differently the next time conflict arises.

CONCLUSION

When we began this study of Emotional Intelligence, I promised you that it would require work. I hope that much is now clear. I also hope you see that this work is doable, that growth is possible, and that improved EI has the power to create meaningful change in every aspect of your life. But it must begin with the self. There is simply no way we can begin the work of connecting with others if we don't begin by connecting with ourselves.

Now that we have covered the three parts of EI—Me, Them, and Us—we're going to get a 10,000 foot view before leaving you with one final challenge to ensure you can keep developing your EI long after you finish reading this book.

To start, let's return to the work we covered together in Part One: Me—Self-Awareness, Self-Control, and Self-Motivation.

SUMMING IT UP—
PART I: ME

Knowing yourself is the beginning of wisdom, according to Aristotle. It's also the beginning of Emotional Intelligence. You should now feel better equipped to check in with yourself, identify what you're feeling, when you're feeling it, and get under the hood of your experience to locate the source of your emotions. If you're having trouble getting specific as you describe what you're feeling, return to the Emotion Wheel in "Chapter 1: Self-Awareness." This will help you drill down into what you're specifically feeling. Remember, just like when you're trying to diagnose a car problem, being as specific as possible is essential for getting to what's really going on inside of you.

Most importantly, you should now be better equipped to control your emotions, rather than letting them control you. When you're feeling overwhelmed, use the tools in "Chapter 2: Self-Control" to help you with this work. Keep in mind, when you're feeling flooded, it's best to step away. Pause for control, take a break when you need it, and then begin again from a place of composure. Another helpful tool to practice before responding to a stressful situation is envisioning the aftermath. Taking the time to imagine different outcomes can help you respond in the most effective way, for yourself and for others.

Central to understanding ourselves is knowing how, and being able to, best motivate ourselves. As we covered in "Chapter 3: Self-Motivation," passions are an important source of motivation. Knowing and making regular time for our passions is one way that we can stay motivated for the long-term.

For some of us, motivation comes from doubling down on a strict routine, and sticking to that structure. For others, we do best with novelty, exploring new activities regularly to encourage inspiration and energy. But, for all of us, we are at our best when we have a diet of both structure and new experiences. One phrase that I hope you will remember is: For every few, do something new. Keep this in mind when you're struggling with motivation.

Relationships are another important source of motivation. These relationships come in many forms: Competition, Accountability, Encouragement. We all need each of these types of motivational relationships in our life, but we're likely to need one more than the others. Remember which relationships are most helpful for your motivation and make sure that you're making regular time for them.

SUMMING IT UP—
PART II: THEM

After we've grown in our understanding of ourselves and our ability to control our own emotions and responses, we move to the work of connecting to 'Them', Part Two of this book. Here's where we covered three essential approaches to connecting: Identifying others' emotions (Chapter 4), Empathizing with others (Chapter 5), and Engaging others' perspectives (Chapter 6).

We can't identify what *others* are feeling until we have done the hard work of identifying what *we're* feeling. But once we have grown in this area of EI, we are better equipped at reading others. And we will be more likely to pick up on how they're feeling through their nonverbal communication.

In addition to reading others, we covered the different ways in which those with a high EI listen curiously and learn more about others. We also covered the ways in which high EI leaders can help reverse and redirect others' negative feelings. Return to "Chapter 4: Identifying" if you need to brush up on any of these skills of identifying with others to connect.

In "Chapter 5: Empathizing," we dug deeper into the central theme of EI: Empathy. Going further than simply identifying what others are feeling, empathy is the ability to feel with others. It is "the fundamental people skill." As we grow in EI, we are better able to empathize with others, realizing a wealth of benefits, not least of which is creating meaningful and deeper connections. Unlike many traits which we either are or aren't born with, empathy is a skill that we can continue to grow in and develop, no matter how naturally it comes to us. By exploring the perspectives of those whose experience is different from our own, and by allowing ourselves to walk in their shoes, we will continue to mature in this central aspect of EI.

Another helpful way to connect with others that I shared with you in "Chapter 6: Engaging," is to fly a kite with the ALAER approach: Ask, Listen, Acknowledge, Explore, and Respond. The more you familiarize yourself with this process, the more natural it will become and you'll quickly find yourself using it in conversations without even thinking about it. It has been a helpful way for me to engage and move beyond surface-level interactions.

So much of what is plaguing our nation today results from a breakdown in our ability to make meaningful connections, especially with those who are different from us. Using the tools in Part Two can help you set a different path for yourself, your family, your staff, and your community.

SUMMING IT UP—
PART III: US

In Part Three: Us, we covered several different levels of connecting with others, from connecting to maintaining to solving.

Not all relationships are equal. "Chapter 7: Connecting" took a deep dive into the five different levels of friendships in our life: Stranger, Acquaintance, Casual Friend, Close Friend, and Intimate Friend. Familiarizing yourself with these different stages will help you distinguish between the different relationships in your life. With some intentionality, you'll be better equipped to move forward in those relationships which you'd like to cultivate to a deeper level.

Social skills can make or break a first impression. Whether it's a first interview or your first time making a presentation to a new client, we covered a range of critical social skills that those with high EI embody to nail a first impression. High EI leaders are always looking for ways to help others improve, and that includes modeling positive social skills in our interactions.

No matter where you are in your EI development, there's always room for improvement. "Chapter 7: Connecting" concluded with a reflection on the four different Communication Styles: Aggressive, Passive, Passive-Aggressive, and Assertive. You should now be able to name your default communication style, be better equipped to navigate them, and to become more assertive.

Relationships require ongoing work. In "Chapter 8: Maintaining," we talked about the importance of maintaining relationships. Speaking from my own experience of friendships that are going on over twenty years, I shared about the importance of showing up for others and being present during crisis events. Often when others are struggling, what they need most from us is simply to be present. From being present with others in their trials to creating a plan to spend regular time together, there are a variety of things those with high EI do in order to maintain those relationships that matter most.

Of course, life happens, and sometimes even meaningful relationships grow distant. When you need to, review "Chapter 8: Maintaining" for tools to help revitalize those relationships that you would like to see thrive once again. And, in those situations where others could use help to manage their negative emotions—whether in the workplace or personal life—we talked about ways those with high EI can create positive outcomes.

Inevitably, conflicts are bound to arise in all but the shallowest relationships. "Chapter 9: Solving" has many of the tools you'll need to navigate, address, and solve trying experiences in relationships: from reframing criticism to delivering hard feedback. All these situations are an opportunity for you to improve and grow and for you to help others do the same. And, when it comes to addressing conflict when it cannot be avoided, make sure you have the helpful three-step approach we covered together to make sure the solution is mutually agreeable for *everyone* involved—that's the only way a solution has any chance of working!

MEASURING EI:
HOW PEOPLE RESPOND TO YOU

In the last chapter, I mentioned the 141 question EI test (MSCEIT) as a measurement of EI. To be honest, there is another way to measure EI. And it's the one that really matters: how other people react to you. How they respond to you. How you make them feel.

If you do not have a positive impact on the people in your life, that is a sure sign that you need to work on your EI. Just as you improve your physical health, just as you improve your mental health, and just as you improve your knowledge, you have to improve your EI. Think of EI as a muscle. If you don't use it, it will atrophy.

> # REMEMBER:
>
> ## THINK OF EI AS A MUSCLE. IF YOU DON'T USE IT, IT WILL ATROPHY.

Believe me, just like your children, your friends and your colleagues notice *everything*. So, humility is the order of the day. Personal accountability is the order of the day. Preserving your values is the order of the day. Remaining calm in a crisis is the order of the day. Being empathetic is the order of the day. And recognizing others' accomplishments with appreciation is the order of the day.

Uphold those orders and everyone will know that you're the walking personification of someone with increasingly high EI.

A FINAL CHALLENGE

One last thing. In order to keep your EI development going long after you put this book down, you've got to consider the role of EI in your daily life. Again, don't let this muscle atrophy—it's far too important!

I challenge you to carry a notepad and a pen with you for a week. Every time you have an interaction with someone, write it down. Then, when you have time, note how you handled the situation. Look back on what happened each day and how you responded.

Did you practice high or low EI? Did you help the person with whom you were interacting with? Did you hurt them? Did they hurt you? Did you hurt or help yourself? What could you have done differently? Most importantly, did you improve over the course of the week? Taking this exercise seriously will help you learn a lot about you and your future self. You may very well decide to keep that notepad and pen with you for much longer than a week!

SOURCES

Elmore, Tim, *Psychology Today*, "The Marks of Maturity," November 14, 2012, https://www.psychologytoday.com/us/blog/artificial-maturity/201211/the-marks-maturity

Goleman, Daniel, *Emotional Intelligence: Why it can matter more than IQ* (New York, Bantam Books, 1997)

Heitler, Susan, *Psychology Today*, "What Makes Conflict? How Are Conflicts Resolved?" November 14, 2012, https://www.psychologytoday.com/us/blog/resolution-not-conflict/201211/what-makes-conflict-how-are-conflicts-resolved

Mayer, John D.; Peter Salovey; and David R. Caruso. *American Psychologist*, "Emotional Intelligence: New Ability or Eclectic Traits?", September 2008, Vol. 63, No. 6, pages 503-517

Moore, Catherine, *Positive Psychology*, "Emotional Intelligence Skills and How to Develop Them," January 9, 2020, https://positivepsychology.com/emotional-intelligence-skills/

Sharma, Shreya, *Bedtime Short Stories*, "Control Your Anger," July 22, 2017, https://www.bedtimeshortstories.com/control-your-anger

Zaki, Jamil, *The New Yorker*, "When Cops Choose Empathy," September 25, 2015, https://www.newyorker.com/tech/annals-of-technology/when-cops-choose-empathy

Chegg Prep, "Emotional Intelligence," https://www.chegg.com/flashcards/emotional-intelligence-ff862768-c00d-40d4-a580-0d558a556b0f/deck?trackid=749c1356e2f0&strackid=af01695e dca2

Help Guide, "Improving Emotional Intelligence," October 2020, https://www.helpguide.org/articles/mental-health/emotional-intelligence-eq.htm

MindTools, "Emotional Intelligence in Leadership: Learning How to Be More Aware," https://www.mindtools.com/pages/article/newLDR_45.htm

Psychology Today, "Emotional Intelligence," https://www.psychologytoday.com/us/basics/emotional-intelligence

Science Daily, "Brain research shows psychopathic criminals do not lack empathy, but fail to use it automatically," July 24, 2013, https://www.sciencedaily.com/releases/2013/07/13072420041 2.htm

ABOUT MIKE ACKER

Mike Acker is a keynote speaker, author, executive, and communication coach with over twenty years of speaking, leadership development, and organizational management experience.

Beyond corporate training, Mike engages in his community as a Seattle TEDx speaker coach and works with international agencies to provide relief amidst poverty.

Mike also enjoys rock-climbing, wake surfing, skiing, church, building Legos with his son Paxton, and going on dates with his wife Taylor. Mike believes in the power of prayer, exercise, journaling, and real community to counter the stresses of everyday life.

http://www.mikeacker.com

CAN YOU HELP?

Can you help? If you liked this book and found it helpful, could you please take a brief moment to review it on Amazon?

Simply visit http://www.amazon.com/author/mikeacker to select *Connect through Emotional Intelligence*. Then leave your honest feedback!

Reviews are extremely important to the success of a book! So if you like what you've read (or even if you didn't), then please take two minutes to help me out with a review. THANK YOU. I appreciate your feedback!

As a big THANK YOU for your review, e-mail contact@ stepstoadvance.com with a link to your *verified* review, and you will get a free 30-minute coaching session with me. There, you can ask me any questions you have about speaking or career advancement!

ALSO BY MIKE ACKER

A Lead with No Fear
In this conversational and action-oriented book, Steve Gutzler and Mike Acker present seven shifts to direct your leadership towards your desired destination: impact, influence, and inspiration.

B Speak with No Fear
Speak With No Fear is the #1 globally highest-ranked book on overcoming the fear of speaking. Full of relatable anecdotes, executable tips, and plenty of laugh-out-loud moments, this book promises to teach you seven proven strategies to help you find your inner presenter.

C Speak with Confidence
Don't just overcome nervousness; discover Mike Acker's proven framework for developing profound confidence to eliminate self-doubt, second-guessing, and weak presence to excel in public speaking and succeed in life.

D Write to Speak
A simple guide to creating content that connects you with your audience. Readers will learn a repeatable system that works for novice and experienced speakers.

E Connect through Emotional Intelligence
In *Connect through Emotional Intelligence*, you will learn to master yourself, avoid disconnection with others, and bridge gaps through increasing your understanding and applying new principles. Increasing your emotional intelligence will improve your relationships, your leadership, and your life.

BOOK MIKE ACKER

FOR YOUR TEAM OR EVENT

Mike Acker is an in-demand keynote speaker on effective communication, emotional intelligence, and transformational leadership. His work in coaching, writing, and speaking inspires audiences around the nation and the globe. His first book, Speak With No Fear, achieved the status of the highest-ranking book on overcoming nervousness in speaking.

He has worked with Adobe, Amazon, Microsoft, Oracle, INOApps, Dallas International School, US Federal Agencies, International Monetary Fund, and many others.

If you are interested in booking Mike Acker for a keynote presentation, workshop, or virtual program, please contact info@mikeacker.com or visit www.MikeAcker.com.

Past Engagements Include: